CARL
ANDRE

By Diane Waldman

The Solomon R. Guggenheim Museum, New York

PUBLISHED BY THE SOLOMON R. GUGGENHEIM FOUNDATION

NEW YORK, 1970

LIBRARY OF CONGRESS CARD CATALOGUE NUMBER: 79 - 138305

LENDERS TO THE EXHIBITION

George H. Andre, Orleans, Massachusetts

Mr. and Mrs. Michael Chapman, New York

Herman and Henriëtte van Eelen, Amsterdam

Mr. and Mrs. Robert A. Feldman, New York

Konrad Fischer, Düsseldorf

Heiner Friedrich, Cologne

Hollis Frampton, New York

Mr. and Mrs. Manuel Greer, New York

Robert Hildt, New York

Mr. and Mrs. Ira Licht, New York

Lee Lozano, New York

Mr. and Mrs. Jan van der Marck, Chicago

Kimiko and John Powers, Aspen, Colorado

Barbara Rose, Madison, Connecticut

Mr. and Mrs. Thomas G. Terbell, Jr., Pasadena

Mr. and Mrs. Herbert Vogel, New York

Aldrich Museum of Contemporary Art, Ridgefield, Connecticut

Brandeis University Art Collection, Waltham, Massachusetts

Hessisches Landesmuseum, Darmstadt, Sammlung Karl Ströher

Milwaukee Art Center Collection

The Museum of Modern Art, New York

National Gallery of Canada, Ottawa

Pasadena Art Museum

Dayton's Gallery 12, Minneapolis

Dwan Gallery, New York

I am grateful to many individuals for their collaboration and support, especially John Weber, Virginia Dwan, Konrad Fischer and Heiner Friedrich, who have been particularly helpful in making this exhibition possible. Kay Epstein and Joanne Bernava of the Dwan Gallery have cooperated in supplying photographs and information for the catalogue. Hollis Frampton has been most generous in allowing his photographs of early Andre works to be used as documentation. I would also like to express my appreciation to Linda Shearer, who worked with me on every phase of the exhibition, and to Douglas Crimp, who aided in the preparation of the catalogue. I am, of course, most grateful to the artist, Carl Andre, for the rewarding experience of working with him at this time.

D. W.

Carl Andre's cryptic definition of sculpture as "FORM = STRUCTURE = PLACE" is significant in clarifying not only his own development but many of the options open to recent contemporary work. Unaccompanied by verbal polemics (in contrast to the de Stijl and Constructivist manifestos, for example), this pronouncement is nevertheless supported by a body of work unshakable in the fervor of its conviction. The conventional role of sculpture as a precious object and its ownership has been rigorously attacked by an oeuvre which refuses, by definition, to make such accommodations.

The concept of place has a profound importance for Andre's work. Its multiple implications disrupted the traditional heroic role of the art object to the extent that Andre's object is viable largely within the context for which it was conceived. The implications of such an ironclad wedding of object to environment are multiple: they presuppose the reductions of the object itself to its lowest point of visibility (hence the word "Minimal"), the denial of the uniqueness of the object as such, without a total rejection of the object which must act as an irritant to the environment and the space that it displaces.

If Andre has retained any convention in his work, it is in the tacit acknowledgement of the fundamental principles of sculpture – mass, space, volume, gravity – while ridding it of traditional form and structure. To this extent, Andre's work has played a germinal role in such recent experiments as Earthworks (for which he expressed an interest as early as 1966) and in the surrender of the object itself (Conceptual Art). Andre's formidable accomplishments occurred in the heady atmosphere of the middle '60's, a time which had not yet begun to question the validity of either the art object per se or its social milieu. Of the sculptors to have emerged in the United States during that period, Andre, together with Robert Morris, Dan Flavin, Sol LeWitt and Donald Judd, can be said to have most successfully defined this position.

Critics writing of Minimal Art, to use a current designation, saw it as a concerted action against the tendencies of Abstract Expressionist sculpture. Such a reaction was inevitable; to propose a radically new sculpture, the entire system of the '50's in art, attitudes and assumptions had to be re-examined. Tentative in supposition, much of the sculpture of the '50's and early '60's, with the notable exception of David Smith, was a painful extension of theories already overextended in painting. Conservative in program, such sculpture seemed constrained to observe conditions which the Minimal sculptors promptly rejected. It was therefore not unexpected that they turned to other sources. That these sources were also derived from painting – the work of Barnett Newman, Ad Reinhardt, Mark Rothko, Jackson Pollock, Jasper Johns and Frank Stella was of particular interest – in no way deterred the manifestation of important '60's sculpture, which Judd once called "specific objects". He wrote in 1965. *"Half or more of the best new work in the last few years has been neither painting nor sculpture"* and *"The new work obviously resembles sculpture more than it does painting, but it is nearer to painting."*[1] The object quality of the structures Judd referred to, however, inspired as it was to a large extent by pictorial precedents of the '50's (although the influence of Constructivism was also a vital factor) matured as a unique composite of illusionistic and three-dimensional devices.

If the '60's sculptors were able to identify with painting, they determined their own position more explicitly in a point-by-point rejection of the more "expressionist" faction of Abstract Expressionism. They opted for interchangeable, mass-produced units, not the conventional methods of hand-made production; for non-relational repetitive forms; for a tough, impassive anonymity in contradiction to the Angst and facture of the '50's; above all, for an art with no ties to representation. The Minimalist focus on mass production and technology was, of course, not new. The early 20th century's fascination with the machine did not, however, extend to the incorporation of actual machine methods but was usually confined to the adaptation of machine forms within a fairly conventional format. And both the Constructivist and Bauhaus experiments were severely hampered by the limited technology and resources available at the time. In a more recent revival of the Dada interest in the machine, Rauschenberg used found objects and silkscreens as a way of removing himself from the picture, and Warhol also confessed his desire to be a machine. Warhol's statement about his paintings reveals several parallel concerns of Pop art and Minimal sculpture, not surprising in that both groups were reacting against Abstract Expressionism:

"I tried doing them by hand, but I find it easier to use a screen. This way, I don't have to work on my objects at all. One of my assistants or anyone else for that matter, can reproduce the design as well as I could."[2]

Compare this with a statement by Sol LeWitt:

"In conceptual art the idea or the concept is the most important aspect of the work. When an artist uses a conceptual form of art, it means that all of the planning and decisions are made beforehand and the execution is a perfunctory affair. The idea becomes a machine that makes the art. This kind of art is not theoretical or illustrative of theories; it is intuitive; it is involved with all types of mental processes and it is purposeless. It is usually free from the dependence on the skill of the artist as a craftsman."[3]

The materials and techniques introduced by both Pop art and Minimal sculpture, while substantively different, are similar in function – to divert, if not actually subvert, tradition. If the connection between the two movements is tangential rather than fundamental, they share what can only be called a Duchampian attitude in their mutual contempt for the sanctity of the art object. The deliberate and flamboyant irony operative in Pop art is muted but just as implicit in Minimal; it varies from the most considered in Morris to the least apparent in Andre and LeWitt; in all cases, it plays a crucial role in conveying ongoing information about the revised role of the object vis-à-vis the artist (and, one might add, the viewer). Where the didactic nature of Pop art consists of the need to render that information viable by the deployment of representational subject matter of the most vulgar kind, in Minimal sculpture it required the exact opposite. For the Minimal sculptors, the need to explain the rejection of the art object as a unique and precious entity culminated in the drastic reduction of the object to its most basic components. That this realization occurred in "specific objects" of extraordinary diversity, encompassing both the illusory and the concrete, is therefore all the more remarkable.

Andre, born in 1935 in Quincy, Mass., studied with Patrick Morgan at the Phillips Academy in Andover, Mass., from 1951-1953, together with Frank Stella and Hollis Frampton, the film-maker. After working briefly for the Boston Gear Works, he left for England and France, visiting Stonehenge, Parliament, the Eiffel Tower and the Louvre, then returned to the States. He spent two years, 1955-1956, as an intelligence analyst with the U.S. Army in North Carolina. In 1957 the moved to New York City and worked as an editorial assistant for a publisher of textbooks. Hollis Frampton, who has documented much of Andre's early development, mentions that at Andover he and Andre shared a mutual interest in poetry; when Frampton arrived in New York early in the spring of 1958 to stay with Andre, he found him living in a cramped hotel room prodigiously at work, chiefly on poetry and occasionally drawings. Another friend left Andre a small apartment that summer and he began at first to make paintings and then sculpture. As Frampton describes that time:

> "The other plastic artists I knew then were 'studio artists', maintaining a workspace and disseminating their work. But CA worked wherever he happened to be, with what was at hand. His studio was his mind, so to speak. Anyone who admired a piece was welcome to shelter it, and a few did, but nothing encumbered him for too long. When he moved, the work was left behind. If it became too copius, he discarded it. Since he has moved often, and produced much, a great deal is gone."[4]

During 1958 Andre produced a number of small sculptures in plexiglas and wood. Drilled and incised, rather than modeled, he kept the alteration of his forms to a minimum, intent on keeping the original block-like surfaces intact. The shapes themselves were strictly geometric – cubes, spheres, cylinders, pyramids, or variations thereon, dictated largely by the nature of the basic cut. Andre then made his first large wood sculptures, man-size "negative sculptures", hand-cut from building timbers. He made these works in Frank Stella's studio, Stella having recently arrived in New York from Princeton. Andre has characterized this time as a period when he was a student of Stella. Taken out of context, this remark assumes a greater significance than it should, but Stella was in fact of great importance to Andre's early development. For example, Stella once remarked to Andre, who was then working on one of his columns cut only on one side, that the untouched rear side was sculpture too. Andre said. "I realized the wood was better before I cut it than after. I did not improve it in any way."[5] He was also quoted as saying:

> "Up to a certain time I was cutting into things. Then I realized that the thing I was cutting was the cut. Rather than cut into the material, I now use the material as the cut in space."[6]

Compare this with Stella's remarks: "I wanted to get the paint out of the can and onto the canvas . . . I tried to keep the paint as good as it was in the can."[7] A Frampton photograph taken in Stella's studio shows one of Andre's wooden columns standing in front of Stella's Union Pacific. It is evident that the internal repetitions of the Andre relate to Stella's painting but Andre's sculpture is, at this juncture, equally indebted to Brancusi. The conspicuous absence of differentiation between sculpture and base is the logical outcome of Andre's prolonged dialogue with Brancusi. Andre has explained the importance of Brancusi's work:

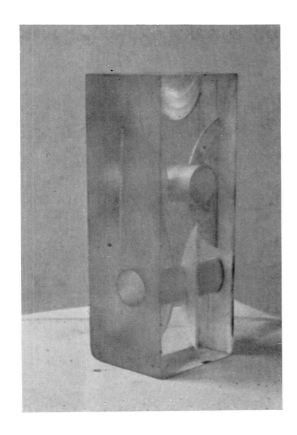

Plexiglas, 1958, Barbara Rose, Madison, Connecticut.

"So Brancusi, to me, is the great link into the earth and the Endless Column is, of course, the absolute culmination of that experience. They reach up and they drive down into the earth with a kind of verticality which is not terminal. Before, that verticality was always terminal: the top of the head and the bottom of the feet were the limits of sculpture. Brancusi's sculpture continued beyond its vertical limit and beyond its earthbound limit. It drove into the earth. Also, Brancusi used many found materials, not that that's important. But he used screws from ancient wine presses and beams pretty much unaltered and combined these particles with those particles that were heterogeneous (not homogeneous). He definitely did combine particles in building up these pedestals which was, for me, the great interest in his work – that those pedestals were the culmination of the materials."[8]

9

Baboons, Winter 1958-59, Lost.

Ladder # 2, Winter 1958-59, Lost.

Untitled, Summer 1959, Lost.

Untitled, Summer 1959, Lost.

Untitled, Summer 1959, Lost.

Although Andre's works of this period continue to reflect Brancusi's influence – in the use of materials, the verticality of form, and in the preference for direct cutting rather than modeling – they do express Andre's insistence on a resolutely abstract form. They can generally be considered anthropomorphic only by association (their verticality), not configuration. Nevertheless, a work like *Ladder 1*, 1959, is residually totemic although the title would appear to deny such connotations. On the other hand, a work such as *Baboons*, also of 1959, while strictly geometric in figuration, is vaguely suggestive of a primate in both the title and the disposition of its members.

Andre gradually enlarged the scale of his wooden pieces, using common-grade lumber mortised together in pyramidal arrangements. Both *Cedar Piece* and *Pyramid*, of 1959, consisted of two identical units which could be rearranged to form an entirely new structure. This factor, in itself, constituted a significant breakthrough for the artist in allowing him to combine his materials without having to model them. It also presupposes an indefinite continuation of the unit like Brancusi's *Endless Column*. The serrated contour of Andre's sculpture resembles the notched forms of a Stella but the work is decidely more original than his previous efforts. The visible evidence of structure, the unaltered surface of his materials, the increased mass and volume were particularly impressive. If the pyramids of 1959 represented a radical

T Piece, 1960, Private Collection, New York (subsequently rearranged, see cat. 8).

Untitled, Winter 1960, Lost.

departure for Andre, they were however still conservative, adhering to some need to grapple with tradition, to create a form (or series of forms) that was memorable and monumental. Andre admitted that *"the vertical element has been the hardest to get away from. Bob Morris and Donald Judd were among the first to break away from the vertical stereotype in sculpture."*[9]

After the bulky monumentality of *Cedar Piece* and the attenuated elegance of *Pyramid*, Andre turned to more modest endeavors. Eschewing both the Brancusi-like column and the Stella-like configurations, he produced a group of small works in plexiglas, wood and metal, which appear to have been an attempt to discover (or recover) basic principles: a T-shaped piece in hot-rolled steel, consisting of two bars simply stacked at right angles to one another; an open frame in wood, a post and lintel structure (titled *Hearth*), etc. These singular experiments lasted for several years; his production from 1960-1964 was limited – partially for lack of funds. He was also working at this time as a freight brakeman and conductor for the Pennsylvania Railroad, an experience that he regards as vital to the development of his sculpture. He worked, as he described it,

" . . . largely in local service in Northern New Jersey to the New Jersey Meadows, where all the highways from the West come into New York. That is vast in scale and not like the plains of the West, but in scale to the urban areas around there. It is an enormous plain with the long lines of freight cars lined up in the freight yards and the flat vast swampy meadows. It just became a strong influence upon my work."[10]

Andre considered his earlier work as *"too architectural, too structural."*[11] From his experience on the railroad, his interest in sculpture changed to become *"more like roads than like buildings."*[12]

Two works of 1964, reconstructed in 1970, appear to have developed out of a renewed consideration of the 1959 pyramids. One, a low horizontal timber piece, has a zigzag contour reminiscent of the stepped indentations of the pyramids. But their ponderous bulk, their absence of embellishment, which extends to the matter-of-fact brutality of the exposed raw ends (like sawed-off limbs), is markedly different from the elegant refinement of *Pyramid*. Andre's decision to splay out a form so that the nature of its making is self-evident (internal and external realities are identical) is a decided contrast to the closed convoluted silhouette of the pyramids. The palpable reminder of a low wall or barrier (like the later styrofoam *Reef*, original 1966; reconstructed 1969, 1970) inevitably suggests analogies to natural forces and the man-made. They also have some bearing on his experience with the railroad in that the timbers are clearly not esthetic in origin, are not manipulated, but are allowed to remain in their original brute-like state. Their presence in a museum context only serves to reinforce the integrity of their initial condition for they act, in effect, in uneasy alliance with their current environment.

In 1965 Andre made still another drastic departure from his earlier work. For an exhibition at the Tibor de Nagy Gallery in New York, he arranged 9-foot long styro-

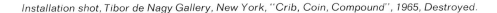

Installation shot, Tibor de Nagy Gallery, New York, "Crib, Coin, Compound", 1965, Destroyed.

foam slabs in three different configurations. Titled *Coin, Compound, Crib* (references to building terms), they were sizable enough to fill most of the gallery, not only disrupting free passage around the work but impeding entry to the main room of the gallery. He had originally set up several timber pieces for the *Shape and Structure* show in early 1965 only to learn that the gallery floor threatened to cave in under their weight. For his subsequent one-man show he turned instead to styrofoam after seeing a friend working with it. The particular qualities of the material, soiled and bruised from handling, conveyed several paradoxical sensations: while fully cognizant of its friable, weightless insubstantiality, one was also aware of the threatening monumentality of the work, especially in proportion to the gallery space. Since it was difficult to gain direct access to the work, from the position of the doorway the three pieces appeared to run together. In this way Andre could demonstrate his reluctance to acknowledge the singularity of a work and concentrate on the greater potential of the environment. If the awareness of the potential for place first appears in these works, it is admittedly tentative; the works demonstrate his continuing reliance on structure, and with it positive and negative spatial relationships; the still perceptible, if inconclusive, differentiation from work to work; and for a residual verticality. The insistence on standard industrial units, soiled and bruised from handling, stacked not glued, became the basis for Andre's later work. Andre's work, in fact, can be dismantled and stored when not on view. In adopting this method for these and later works, Andre laid claim to the use of regimented, interchangeable units, which only assume an identity when the need arises to set up or reconstitute a work.

Installation shot, Tibor de Nagy Gallery, New York, "Equivalents", 1966.

Andre's decision to make his sculptures hug the ground was finalized in the summer of 1965 when he was canoeing on a lake in New Hampshire: it became apparent to him that his work should be as level as water. For his next exhibition at the de Nagy Gallery Andre worked directly on the floor, laying out a group of sand lime bricks in units of 120. Stacked in two layers to prevent drift, each of the four permutations – 3 x 20, 4 x 15, 5 x 12, 6 x 10 – resulted in eight substantially different works (the bricks were aligned either by length or width, hence the eight combinations). Given the four combinations, the visual differences were striking. In 1967, at the Dwan Gallery in Los Angeles, Andre laid out a floor of concrete bricks into which cuts, roughly approximating the brick pieces of the de Nagy exhibition in reverse, were made into the "floor". Although Andre's concern for environment figured importantly in his previous exhibitions at the de Nagy Gallery, at the Dwan Gallery he totally eliminated the object (except as a negative sculpture) in favor of the allover situation. Titles for the two exhibitions, *Equivalents* (de Nagy, 1966) and *Cuts* (Dwan, 1967) make specific the different directions in which he was working. Works like *Equivalents*, *Cuts* and the more recent *Five Corners* that he executed for the Ace Gallery in Los Angeles in 1970 have prompted comparisons to Constructivism. Apart from the fact that Andre, like the other Minimalists, openly acknowledges in his work an affinity to Constructivism, the context has been so altered as to render such a designation meaningless (or peripheral at best). Of the three works just cited, *Five Corners* bears the most explicit reference to Constructivism, to Malevitch's *White on White* painting of 1918. The more than casual relationship to pictorialism

Installation shot, Dwan Gallery, Los Angeles, "Cuts", 1967.

Installation shot, Tibor de Nagy Gallery, New York, 1966.

Installation shot, Ace Gallery, Los Angeles, "Five Corners", 1970.

Windham College, Putney, Vermont, "Joint", 1968.

has an equally effective counterpoint in the physical properties of the work: the location of the work and the spectator's response to both the work and the environment ultimately refute such associations. The most dynamic single aspect of the work is the fact that Andre reverses what could be construed as a figure-ground relationship: by activating the corners of the room (with his metal plates), he not only stresses the relationship of the work to the room but stabilizes it.

The single most radical work of Andre's, prior to the metal plate pieces, was *Lever*, 1966, a single row of 137 unattached firebricks, installed in the Jewish Museum in such a way that the viewer could approach it from either of two directions. From one position, it was possible to view the entire length of the work in receding perspective. From another doorway, only the terminal portion was visible. Because of the unusual length of the work, which disrupted the flow of traffic, it was impossible to reconstruct the work satisfactorily from all angles. *Lever* was jarring in its total lack of convention; not only in terms of materials, the lack of any apparent structure, but in the absence of one correct perspective or focus. In speaking about the radical change in his work, Andre said,

> "... all I am doing is putting Brancusi's Endless Column on the ground instead of in the air. Most sculpture is priapic with the male organ in the air. In my work Priapus is down to the floor. The engaged position is to run along the earth."[13]

Lever, projecting from one wall of the Jewish Museum, represented yet another phase in Andre's progression towards place; that is, it was still partially engaged with the wall.

Andre realized the full potential of place with his metal-plate pieces begun in 1967, but in the interim he experimented with several possibilities – a scatter piece, *Spill*; a pile of sand deposited in the Museum of Contemporary Crafts – and indicated an interest in Earthworks mentioning that his *"ideal piece of sculpture is a road."*[14] *Spill*, a work whose dimensions could only be determined when the 800 identical

Installation shot, Haags Gemeentemuseum, 1969.

plastic blocks were removed from their canvas bag and flung onto the floor, evidenced a Pollock-like quality in their overall randomness. *"The particles are so small they don't make a coherent pattern. The small size dictates a less rigid form. The random spill makes the pattern."*[15] Andre demonstrated with these works some interest in process (time) and in work that was distinctly anti-form; he also evinced some reluctance to give up the basic geometric unit so important to his desires.

Like the brick pieces before them and the styrofoam slabs, Andre's metal plates are standard commercial units, identical modules determined in number by simple arithmetic combinations. The use of modular methods is common to much Minimal art but Andre has resisted the tendency apparent in the work of most of the other leading sculptors in the idiom to wrest a configuration from them. In almost every instance the work is resolutely square. In spite of Andre's insistence on regularity of form, each work is sufficiently different in details to command renewed attention. Andre's obsessiveness is, in this respect, like Mondrian's; given his decision to work with just a few fundamental principles, the variety of possibilities is enormous.

37 Pieces of Work occupies approximately 36 x 36' of the ground floor of the Guggenheim Museum. It is composed of 1296 units: 216 each of aluminium, copper, steel, magnesium, lead and zinc. The title incorporates not only the one 36' square but a projected series of 36 works, each 6 x 6' and consisting of 36 units of the same materials as the large work. Of Andre's metal-plate pieces from 1967 to the present, *37 Pieces of Work* is the most complicated in its admixture of elements. In its relationship to the museum, it works not only with the floor plane but with the full height and breadth of the museum's structure. If one considers the Guggenheim Museum as the progression of a series of curves and arcs, then it is possible to see Andre's *37 Pieces of Work* as a conscious interruption of that sequence. The harmonious balance of the spiral – its particular forms, textures and nuances – has been so altered by the Andre as to render the space anew. Even more significant is the fact that the Wright structure offers Andre a unique opportunity to coordinate all of the factors which occupy his concept of place and the result is monumental, not only in terms of scale, of which he is a master, but in terms of the opulence and play of his materials. As such, the work radiates an extraordinary play of light that is almost Byzantine in its splendor.

Andre's work for the Haags Gemeentemuseum in the fall of 1969 indicated his continuing obsession with place. For this occasion, however, the emphasis was not on a rectangular configuration but on a linear one. Like Andre's other floor pieces, they were intended for a particular situation. The repetition of the pattern of the floor of the museum was given due consideration and Andre decided to work both in and around it. Although these pieces give the impression of line, they are small commercial units, three dimensional in fact. In these bent-pipe and nail pieces Andre is exploring just how far he can go in diminishing the physical substance of a work without destroying its presence; he is also determining how far he can reduce his form and still hold the floor. By placing his work directly on the floor Andre makes us aware of gravity as a condition of sculpture, not by struggling with it but by proximity.

To the extent that Andre uses the visual plane, there remains some residue of pictorial illusionism; but the very real presence of the work is reinforced by several factors: the physical reality of the mental plates; the very real differences of surface, texture, and colors of the materials of such elementary substances as lead and zinc; the possibility of walking on the pieces; time – the natural process of allowing his materials to weather, decay, rust, etc. Since a work is specifically placed, at least in its original situation, it follows that the particular relationship to place, if the work were successful, would make one aware of all the facets of that relationship. Andre, in forcing us to engage his work directly, by physical contact, a sensation that is always initially disorienting, encourages us to acknowledge our own existence first of all. This awareness, and the subsequent identification with his work, has the cumulative effect of forcing a recognition of nature. By respecting not only the inherent properties of his materials but also the given situation of specific environment, Andre has been able to elicit a body of work that is remarkable in both its cohesiveness and its consistency.

Although Andre's work is resolutely concrete, and aspires to document no condition other than its own existence, it has one fundamental characteristic that differentiates it quite explicitly from the work of other Minimalists: it identifies with nature, not in form but in its recognition of the floor as a zone for existence. If his understanding of Brancusi was vital to this process, then the work of Frank Lloyd Wright served as further reinforcement. The transformation of nature, in both Wright and Brancusi, found a counterpart in Andre in his adherence to place as the focal point of man and nature. One could say that Andre has given up everything and yet he has given up nothing – in an art with no overt references to life, his work is all the more real. Unlike Pop art, which must of necessity make explicit its references to the real world, and is thereby constrained to deal only with the present, Andre's art is free (of those limitations) to dwell upon the fundamental sources of reality.

Artist's Studio, New York, Spring 1970.

1   Donald Judd, "Specific Objects", *Arts Yearbook*, 8, 1965, pp. 74, 77.

2   Andy Warhol in *Andy Warhol*, exhibition catalogue, Neue Nationalgalerie, Berlin, March 1-April 14, 1969, n.p.

3   Sol LeWitt, "Paragraphs on Conceptual Art", *Artforum*, V/10, Summer 1967, p. 80.

4   Hollis Frampton, "Letter to Enno Develing", in *Carl Andre*, exhibition catalogue, Haags Gemeentemuseum, August 23-October 5, 1969, p. 8.

5   Enno Develing, essay in *Carl Andre*, exhibition catalogue, Haags Gemeentemuseum, August 23-October 5, 1969, p. 39.

6   David Bourdon, "The Razed Sites of Carl Andre: A Sculptor Laid Low by the Brancusi Syndrome", *Artforum*, V/2, October 1966, p. 15.

7   "Questions to Stella and Judd", *Art News*, 65/5, September 1966, p. 58. Interview by Bruce Glaser; edited by Lucy L. Lippard. (Discussion originally broadcast on WBAI-FM, New York, February 1964 as "New Nihilism or New Art?")

8   "An Interview with Carl Andre", *Artforum*, VIII/10, June 1970, p. 61. Interview by Phyllis Tuchman.

9   "Andre: Artist of Transportation", *The Aspen Times* (Colorado), July 18, 1968. Interview by Dodie Gust.

10   Enno Develing, op. cit., p. 40.

11   Interview with Dodie Gust, op. cit.

12   Ibid.

13   Enno Develing, op. cit., p. 40.

14   David Bourdon, op. cit., p. 17.

15   Interview with Dodie Gust, op. cit.

SCULPTURE

1   Ladder # 1, 1958.

2 Plexiglas and Wood, 1958-59.

3   Wooden Piece, 1959.

4　Pyramid, original 1959; reconstruction 1970.

5   Cedar Piece, original 1959; reconstruction 1964.

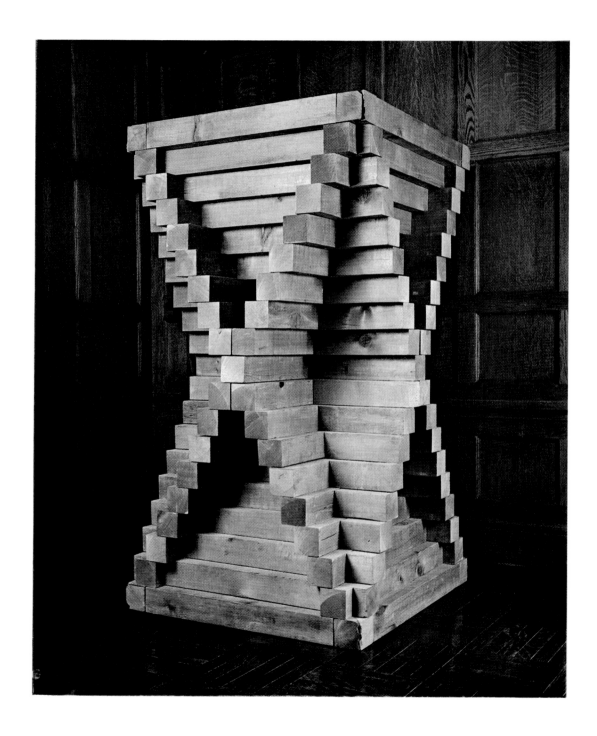

6 Untitled, 1960.

7 Untitled, 1961.

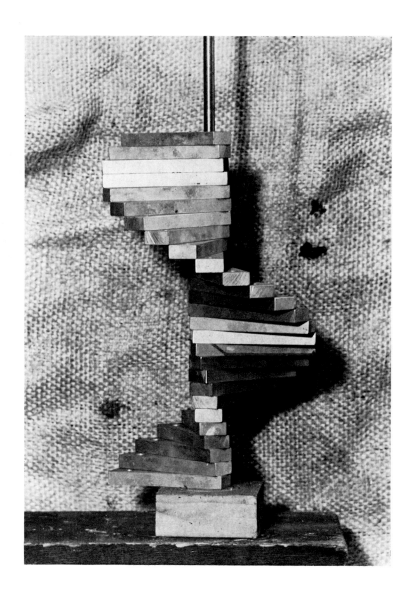

8   Steel Piece, Spring 1961.

9   Hourglass, 1962.

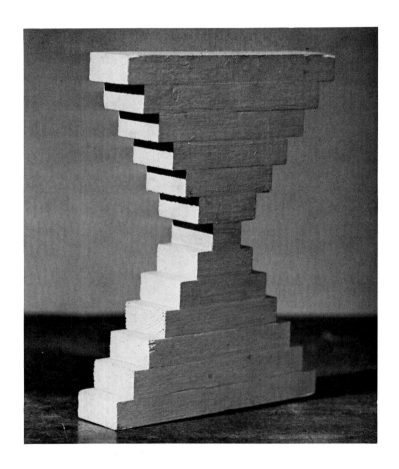

10   Cock, 1963.

11 Chain Sculpture, 1964.

12a   Timber Piece, original 1964; reconstruction 1970.

12b   Timber Piece, original 1964; reconstruction 1970.

13   Untitled, 1965.

14   Equivalent, 1966.

15   Equivalent, original 1966; reconstruction 1969.

16　Lever, original 1966; reconstruction 1969.　　　　　17　Reef, original 1966; reconstruction 1969, 1970.

18   Spill (Scatter Piece), 1966.

19 12 Pieces of Steel, 1967.   20 Steel Piece, 1967.

21   144 Steel Plates, 1967.

22   144 Aluminium Plates, 1967.

23   144 Zinc Plates, 1967.   24   Fall, 1968.

25   144 Lead Plates, Spring 1969.

26   144 Magnesium Plates, Spring 1969.

28   64 Pieces of Copper, Spring 1969.

Copper "Ribbon" Piece, Summer 1969 (left)   29   Alluminium "Ribbon" Piece, Summer 1969 (right)
Collection G. J. Visser, Antwerp.
Not in exhibition

30   17 Steel Rod Run, Summer 1969.

31   Alloy Square, Fall 1969.

1859

DUTY OF WATER: GORKY

WHITE MEN
CRIMSON CROSS
ON THE
SETTLED BY
TERRITORY

VERY LARGE BLACK
COAL-BLACK
& HIS HAIR IS
NO RIGHTS WHICH
MAGNIFY THE HAPPINESS

BLUE ATMOSPHERE
CLOSING FIELDS OF
THE RED NOSE
FUN PINCH THE
WHITES & BLACKS

HUES WHICH MOCK
SO BLUE LIPS
THY GOLDEN HAIR
A LOCK OF THY
IN A BLACK BRAID MET

HAG SHE TURNED
FROM WASHINGTON
UNDER LIEUT. ISRAEL
GREEN A DRAGON
GREEN MARINES

IN THE ARMORY
BROWN IS DYED
HIS ROSE WREATH
TRIBE BENEATH
ARCHED THE RAINBOW

OF THE PROVINCIAL
GOVERNMENT OF THE
ARMY IN CHIEF
BROWN COMMANDER
OLD OSAWATOMIE

BY THE BLUE RIDGE
BEEN DAMMED UP
THE GAP THROUGH WHICH
CLOSING FIELDS
ARRANGED & COLOURED

RED WITH RAGE
WHITES & BLACKS
COLOURS THE SCENE
THE RICHMOND GREYS
SEEMED TO BE BLACK

move us to the cool chalk-like what clarity

over all tortures where once great centuries

danced celtic with gaiety bleeds on thy mouth

of me in paradises

apricots shape apricots dependent breasts

deprived of leaves was the Holy Tree of their

clothes banners under pressure to the sh-h-h-sh-h

isle of Manhattan

to dissect an aeroplane the sensation of

the passengers my panel of the first balloon

becomes green is black on beholding the anatomical

parts of autogyros

is black the rudder yellow toys of men as

children of a meteor cleaving the art business

without my Mougouch having the measles

vegetables and fruit

of four chimpanzees old men without dispute

giving bread & carrots of a lovely man with this

hairy mass of monkey flesh mask of chimpanzees

covered with hideous fur

the grass sister mother in the same bed of April

& May making Chelbour & also lentil soup to work

into your body fearfully linked cardinal liver

mirrors saliva

white chalk white angels black angels move in

opposed directions inflict Mougouch's ears

cutting an egg hovering the snake so exactl

trickling onto black & white

ah	ambassadors	am	ayagualulco	as
all	accomplish	add	accordance	are
arms	affection	army	artillery	burn
alert	brothers	beads	artifice	beach
ascent	anxiety	attack	cacique	banner
battles	bishop	cavalry	christ	brother
audacity	anger	disaster	brawl	boulders
daughters	city	ancestors	fear	followers
assistance	but	astonished	beg	christians
confinement	be	foolishness	by	disturbance
conclusion	bad	confidence	dog	conscience
gentlemen	duty	chieftain	evil	hardships
boldness	cloth	fortress	curse	children
courage	cortes	emperor	danger	baggage
defeat	husband	devils	kinsmen	famine
death	dishonor	cross	feathers	jesus
gold	montezuma	face	gatherers	bone
cry	expedition	act	disservice	get
go	exterminate	he	distinction	if
god	encounters	how	friendship	cue
food	ignorance	gods	lightning	fury
night	creation	lance	garrison	death
dagger	parrots	jewels	infante	horses
justice	mother	mantles	cortes	opinion
nonsense	maize	horsemen	plume	drinking
montezuma	gift	necessity	kill	multitude
chieftains	men	fortresses	not	possession
huichilobos	it	improvement	me	misfortunes
sacrifices	pay	moderation	law	musketeers
ornaments	guns	knowledge	lady	montezuma
mischief	rites	musician	mercy	nobility
dollars	pardon	majesty	fright	marches
mexico	muskets	nephew	sierras	mantle
power	opponent	padre	treasure	sleep
ears	mountains	mare	sacrifice	mock
hut	themselves	eye	pestilence	god
no	crossbowmen	on	malefactors	or
man	punishment	run	reputation	sea
rags	nonentity	shot	obedience	skin
stone	shoulder	spain	password	trees
sierra	ravings	palace	sunrise	slaves
shelter	silver	traitor	speech	straits
stallion	truth	religion	valor	surprise
squadrons	sign	prisoners	stab	spaniards
protection	son	stratagems	tax	throughout
opportunity	no	soothsayers	or	possibility
tlaxcalans	war	touchstone	way	victorious
suffering	town	victories	wars	vassalage
soldiers	winds	strength	wives	thoughts
voyages	savage	welcome	silver	tribute
strike	warfare	towers	worship	wounds
words	warriors	wound	watchmen	world
year	surrender	wood	turbulent	work
war	wickedness	yet	yourselves	why
so	opportunity	we	tezcatepuca	up

CONQUESTDISPLAYOCTOBER1965ANDRE

34   Touch Power, 1965.

BLACK	DROWN	BAN	WHITE	LIFE	BAY
CHEESE	NAIL	SUN	POT	WAR	MAN
ACT	ICE	DRAG	DREAM	BEER	PLANT
OWL	BAR	STORM	GHOST	LUMP	FORCE
HOPE	RING	CLUB	CROWN	BOY	SHINE
BITE	PASTE	BOOK	SNAKE	GLOOM	SMELL
RHYME	ARMS	SCALE	BITCH	HASP	THORN
BACK	STAR	FAN	SOURCE	COW	AX
WAX	CRAMP	TIME	BOX	RUST	FLY
FEET	SKY	TOOTH	EGG	DEATH	SCOPE
TEAR	FAST	CHANGE	SNAIL	LUNG	CRAB
HOOK	SOIL	MOUTH	FIRE	JOY	RED
HAND	GRID	FATE	BREAD	CORK	THUMB
MILK	SHORE	GLASS	HELL	CASE	BLUFF
ROACH	CART	SPIT	BRAIN	SPRING	POUND
CLOUD	STONE	LOOM	MOUSE	STRIKE	ZONE

36   Structure White Consciousness, 1965.

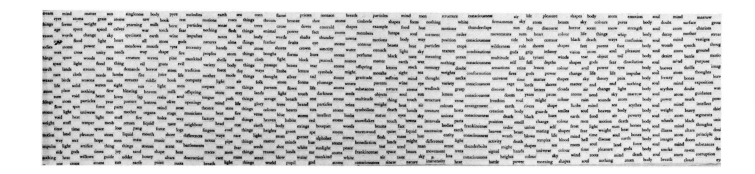

limbs boy woman
hand body human breathing
man air forms day heat seed charm
heat seed water fire itself fire sun manhood
flame spring magnet night atom spring ambrosia dart
beacon ice forms torch spring earth heat wound
foe sickness heat stone water mariners stone breeze iron blood
human daylight laws path iron sun chain blaze skin love
morsel earth fountain stone spot atoms parts waves fire man
plant sponge chain heat ring air stone
nectar fire sky heat tinder water iron things brass stream gold olive
delight skin water wick seeds sea brass sails parts desires heat wax flesh
temper earth energy fire hand turmoil pores air magnet water sun bronze
goats iron fountain rings bubble iron ring time ships stone lamp snow
pigs flesh breezes magnet rings object frame spring sky
sense world fire hand torch stone all air things fire forms love
man atom spring abode country myself iron space motion taper surface
things bottom light stone dance things wind doubt stone tinder
ground way iron power soil iron bowl ring iron wonder water
sun race strength atom sea stone air spring fire
hills nothing sky water taper pores spring itself atom
particles fact earth iron way tinder earth waters
power things spring stone seeds torches heat forms
ice earth bodies texture things power atom
energy beasts surge fire rays frost breath fire
atoms men spring forms water walls
way stone torch breath heat
causes heat man
boys ointment limbs
love impulse
mind

38   Bulk Cake, 1965.

```
B U L K C A K E C E L L C H I P C O I N C U R B D E C K
D E E D D I R T D I S K D O C K D O M E D O O R
E D G E F A C E F A R M F E E T F I L E F I L M F I R E
F L A G F L O W F O I L F O O T F O R M F R O G G A T E G L O W
G O L D G U L F H A L L H A N D H E A D H E A P H E A T
H E E L H I L L H O L E H O O F H U S K K I S S L A K E K N E E
L A K E L A M P L A N D L A W N L E A D L E A F L I N E
L I N K L I S T L O C K L U M P M A R K M A S K M A S S
M I L E M I L L M I N D M I N E M I N T M O D E M O S S
N A I L N A M E N I N E N O O N N O T E N O U N P A C E
P A L M P A N E P A R K P A R T P A T H P E A K P E E L
P I E R P I L E P I L L P L A N P L O T P L O W P O L E
P O O L P O R E P O R T P O S T P R O P R A C E R A C K
R A I L R A I N R A N K R A T E R E E F R E I N R E S T
R I N G R I T E R O A D R O C K R O O F R O O M R O O T
R O P E R O S E R U L E R U N G R U S T S A C K S A I L
S A N D S C A R S E A L S E A M S E A T S E E D S H E D
S H I P S H O E S I D E S I G N S I L K S I T E S I Z E
S L A B S N O W S O I L S P A N S P I N S P I T S P O T
S P U R S T A R S T E M S T E P S T O P S U I T S W A Y
T A I L T A P E T A S K T E R M T E X T T H A W T I C K
T I D E T I L E T I M E T I N T T I L T T I L L T I R E
T O I L T O M B T O N E T O O L T O W N T R A P T R A Y
T R E E T R I M T U B E T U C K T U F T T U R N T U N E
T U R N T W I G T Y P E U R G E V A S E V E I L V E I N
V E N T V E R B V I E W V I N E V O I D V O L T W A G E
W A L L W A N D W A R D W A R E W A R P W A S H W A S P
W A V E W E E D W E L L W H I P W I L L W I N D W I N E
W O O D W O R D W O R K Y A R D Y A R N Y O K E Z O N E
```

63

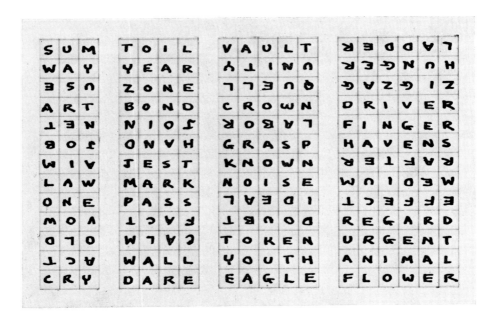

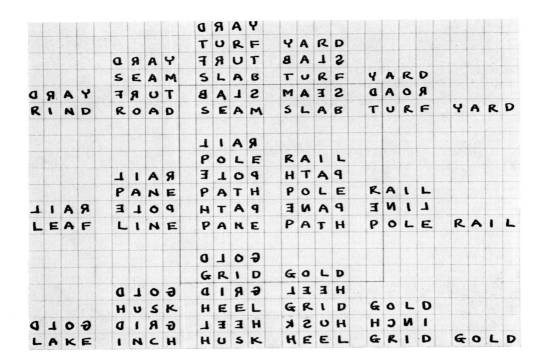

41   Impulse Driver, 1965.

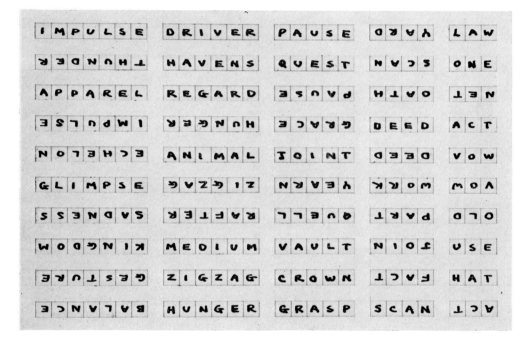

42   Flags, 1964.

FLAGS

AN OPERA FOR THREE VOICES

TO DE KOONING

    POLLACK

    GORKY

3-31-64

1
FLAGS

```
     I: WORKING WOMEN  WOMEN  WOMEN  WOMEN  WOMEN  WOMEN  WOMEN  WOMEN  WOMEN  WOMAN  WOMAN
 1)  II:
     III:                                                                          TREE

     I: WOMAN      WOMAN      WOMAN      WOMAN      WOMAN      WOMAN      WOMAN
 2)  II:
     III:    THREE      THEY       THE        THE        THE        THE      AWAY  THE

     I: WOMAN      WOMAN                       WOMAN                      WOMAN
 3)  II:                              WYOMING                  TRIPTYCH  WOUNDED
     III:    AT  THE     ARTIST'S PORTRAIT  THE        ARTIST  PORTRAIT  THE

     I:           STREET     WOMAN                 STREET      WOMAN
 4)  II:                 TOTEM  WOODEN               TOTEM  WOMAN
     III: ARTICHOKE  PORTRAIT      THE      ARGULA  PORTRAIT       THE       ANTIQUE

     I: MORN       STREET     WOMAN   MORAINE                       STENOGRAPHER
 5)  II:           SYMBOL TOTEM WOMAN                               SUMMERTIME
     III:    OWL  PORTRAIT      THE      AND       ORGANIZATION  PORTRAIT
```

2
FLAGS

```
     I: TWO   WOMAN     MONTAUK             STANDING  TWO    WOMAN
 6)  II: THREE  WOMAN                       SUBSTANCE THERE  WOMAN
     III: THE       AND        ORATORS  PORTRAIT SUNSET  THE       AND  COMPOSITION

     I: MONDAY          STANDING  TWO  WOMAN                 MERRITT
 7)  II:           SOUNDS    THE   WOLF  AUTUMN
     III:    OF  PORTRAIT  SUN     THE      AND    COMPOSITION ISLAND MYSELF  OF  PLOW

     I: STANDING  TWO  WOMAN                  MEN      SQUARE   TWO  WOMAN
 8)  II: SQUARE    THE  WHITE  ARABESQUE               SLEEPING THE  WHITE
     III: SUN      THE       ANCESTOR  COMPOSITION IS LOVE MY OF PLACE SUMMATION THE WITH

     I: AUGUST                        MATCH      SITTING  TWO  WOMAN ATTIC
 9)  II: ANIMAL              FULL                 SILVER   THE  WHITE ANGEL
     III: ANATOMICAL BULL COMPANION    IS LIVER MY OF PIRATE STILL  THE  WITH  AN

     I:                      MARSHES       SEPTEMBER TWO  WOMAN ATTIC BROWN
10)  II:          FROGMAN    MURAL         SILVER    THE  WHITE AND   BROWN
     III: BROWN  COMBAT         IN LINCOLN MY  OF PIRATE STILL THE WITH AN BOY

     I:                  MANNEQUINS      SELF  TWO  WOMAN ASHVILLE BROTHER
11)  II: CUTS  FRIEZE    MURAL     OUT    SILVER THE WHITE AND   BLUE
     III: COMB       IN LIMIT MY    OF PERSONAGE STILL THE WITH AHKO  BLACKBOARD
```

```
        I:                      MAN         ORESTES          SEATED    TIME  WOMAN  AS    BOUDOIR
12) II:  CUT      FOUR          MOON        OUT                SHIMMERING  THE  WHITE  AND  BLUE
   III:  COCK'S   IN  LIFE  MY  NUDE  OF    PALETTE  STILL     THE        WITH  AGONY  BILL


        I:        FRIDAY             LITTLE  MAN          OPEN     PORTRAIT  SEATED  THREE
13) II:  CONVERGENCE  FOR  GUARDIANS        MOON         ORANGE              SHE     THE
   III:  CHILD'S          GUN    IN  LIFE  MOTHER'S  NUDE  OF  PALETTE  SONG  THE


        I:  WOMAN  ANGELS    BOUDOIR             FOREST              ISLAND  LIGHT  MAN    NUDE
14) II:  WHITE  AND  BLACK    CODY  EYES  FLAME  GREEN  HORSE                MIST
   III:  WILL   AFTERNOON  BETROTHAL  CHILD      FROM   GREEN   IN    LIFE  MOTHER  NOSTALGIA


        I:  ON     POND   SEATED  THE  WITH  AND    BOOK                              FIRST
15) II:  OPPOSITES        SEVEN   THE  WHITE  AND    BLACK    COCKATOO  DREAM  EYES  FIVE
   III:  OF     PAINTING  SOFT   THE  WIFE  ABSTRACTION  BETROTHAL  CHARRED          FLOWERY


        I:  GREEN          INTERCHANGE  LEAVES  MAN  NOON      ON   POND    SEATED  THE
16) II:  GREEN  HORIZONTAL     .            MIST          ONE   PROCEEDS  SECRET  THE
   III:  GRAY   HOW     IN        LIFE  MRS  NINETEENFORTYFOUR  OF  PAINTING  SOCHI  THE


        I:  WHITE  AND  BOLTON                  FIRE     GOTHAM            INCIDENT
17) II:  THERE  AND  BLACK   CIRCLE  DEPOSITION  EIGHT  FIGURES  GRAYNESS  HEAT
   III:  WIFE   A    BELOVED  CHARRED                    FLOWERS  GOOD     HOUSATONIC  IMPATIENCE
```

```
        I:  LANDSCAPE  MAN    NIGHT      OF  POLICE            SEATED  THE  WHARF     ACROBAT  BLACK
18) II:           MIRROR  NIGHT      ON  PORTRAIT  RITUAL  SCENT   THE  WEB       AND      BLACK
   III:  LEAF       MILL   NIGHTTIME  OF  PAINTING          SKULL   THE  WATERFALL  A        BELOVED


        I:      DUCK   EXCAVATION  FIRE       GLAZIER       IN       JULY  LANDING  MAN   NIGHT
19) II:  CHILD  DEEP   EFFORT      FIGURE     GRAYED   HEAT  IN            MASK      NIGHT
   III:  CAST   DIARY  ENIGMATIC   FIREPLACE  GOLDEN   HIS   IMAGINARY    LAST  MASTER  NIGHT


        I:  OF  PINK           SATURDAY  THE  WEEHAWKEN  A  BICYCLE  CORNER     DEATH     ELEGY
20) II:  OF  PORTRAIT  RHYTHM  SEASCAPE  THE  WAR        A  BIRTH    CEREMONY  DEBUTANTE  ECHO
   III:  OF  PAINTING          SELF      THE  WATERFALL  A  BATTLE   CALENDARS  DERVISH   ENIGMA


        I:  FIGURE  GAZETTE    IN     JANUARY  LADY    MALE                    WAVE    ZURICH
21) II:  FEMALE  GRAY    HEAD   IN            LIGHT   MALE  UNFORMED          WATER
   III:  FAR     GOD     HIGH   IMAGE          LANDSCAPE  MAKING  UNFOLDS  VIRGINIA  WATER


        I:  A  BACKYARD  CLASSIC    DARK   EASTER          FEBRUARY  GANSEVOORT  HIGHWAY  IMAGINARY  JANUARY
22) II:  A  BIRD      CATHEDRAL  DANCER  EASTER          FATHOM    GOTHIC      HEAD     IN
   III:  A  BACKBONE  CALENDAR   DARK   EMBROIDERED  FALLS        GARDEN      HEAD     IDUMEAN


        I:      LADY     MAILBOX  NETHERLANDS  OCHER     PARKWAY  ROAD      SAGAMORE  TENTH
23) II:  KEY  LAVENDER  MAGIC    NIGHT        OCEAN   PASIPHAE  RAINBOW  SEARCH   THE       UNCONSCIOUS
   III:       LANDSCAPE  MAIZE    NEW          OBJECTS  PAINTING  ROSES    SEDUCER  TABLE     UNATTAINABLE
```

```
        I:  VALENTINE  WAREHOUSE        ZOGBAUM
24) II:  VIBRATIONS  WAGON
   III:  VARTOOSH   WAS     XHORKOM
                                        (END)
```

67

43   Names, 1964.

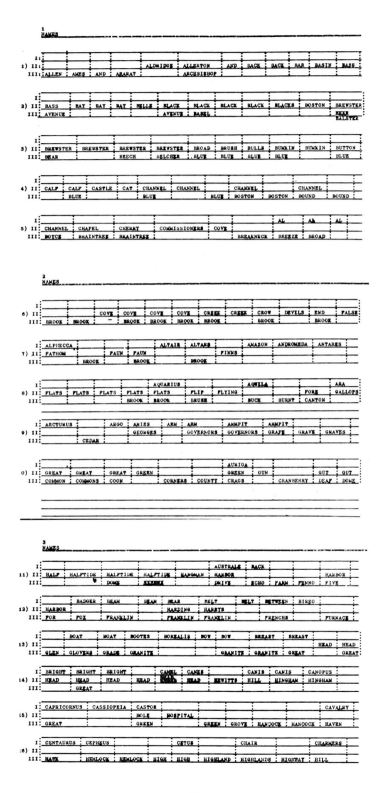

NAMES

17)

I:	CITY		CLAW	CLAW		COLUMBA	CORONA	CORVUS	CRAB	CROWN
II:		HULL	HULL	HUNT	HYPOCRITE		HYPOCRITE	INLET		INNER
III:		HILL	HILL	HILL	HILL		HILL			HILL

18)

I:	CRUX	CYGNUS	DAM	DAUGHTERS	DELPHINUS	DEMONS	DESOLATE	DHIRAH	DIM	DOG
II:	INNER	ISLAND	ISLAND	ISLAND	ISLAND	ISLAND	ISLAND	ISLAND	ISLAND	ISLAND
III:	HILL	HILL								

19)

I:	DOG				DOLPHINS	DRACO	DRAGONS	EAGLES		KAM	ELBOW
II:	ISLAND	ISLAND	ISLAND				ISLAND		ISLAND		
III:	HILL			HILL					HILL		HILL

20)

I:	END	ERIDANUS	FIRST	FISHES	FLOCK	FOLLOWER	FOLLOWING			FOOT
II:		ISLAND	ISLAND	HILL						ISLAND
III:			HILL	HILL	HILL	HILL		HILL	HILL	HILL

21)

I:		FOOT	FOOTSTOOL	FOREHEAD	FORTUNATE	GATE	GATE	GATHERER		
II:	ISLAND		ISLAND	ISLAND	ISLAND	ISLAND		ISLAND		ISLAND
III:			HILLS	HILLS	HILLS	HILLSIDE		HILLSIDE		HOLBROOK

22)

I:	GEMINI	GIRDLE	GOAT	GOATS	GOLDFISH		GRAPE	GREAT	GRUS	HAM	HAND
II:		ISLAND		ISLAND	ISLAND		ISLAND				
III:	HOLBROOK		HOLE		HOLLINGSWORTH	HOLLOW			HOLY		

NAMES

23)

I:	HAND	HAND	HAND	HARE	HEAD	HEAD	HEAD	HEAD	HEAD	HEART
II:	ISLAND	ISLAND	ISLAND	ISLAND	ISLAND			ISLAND	ISLAND	
III:		HOSPITAL	HOUGHTON			IN	IN	INDEPENDENCE		

24)

I:	HEEL	HENS	HERCULES	HIGH	HIND	HO	HORN		HORN		
II:	ISLAND	ISLAND	ISLAND	ISLAND	ISLAND			ISLAND	ISLE	JACKKNIFE	KELLY
III:		INDIAN									

25)

I:				HORSES	HYAENA	HYDRA	HYDRUS			INDI
II:		KELP	KING			LANGLEE				
III:	INTERCHANGE			INTERCHANGE			JOHNS	JOSEPHS	KING	

26)

I:		INNER	KING	KNEE	KNEE	KNEELERS		KNOT		KNOT	LEFT
II:			LEDGE	LEDGE	LEDGE	LEDGE	LEDGE	LEDGE			LEDGE
III:	KITCHAMAKIN	LAKE		LAKE	LAKE	LAKE				LANE	LEDGE

27)

I:	LEFT	LEG		LEO	LEPUS	LIBRA	LINCHPIN	LIONS	LITTLE	LOIN
II:	LEDGE	LEDGE		LEDGE	LEDGE			LEDGE	LEDGE	LEDGE
III:	LIBERTY	LIBERTY	LIBERTY			LIBRARY	LINWOOD	LODGE		MAIN

28)

I:		LOIN		LUCKIEST	LUCKIEST	LUCKY	LUCKY	LUPUS	LYNCIS	LYRA	MAJOR
II:	LEDGE	LEDGE			LEDGE	LEDGE	LEDGE	LEDGES	LITTLE		LITTLE
III:	MAIN		MAPLE	MAPLEWOOD	MARTIN			MARYS		MEADOW	

NAMES

29)

I:	MANE	MARCHER				MIAPLACIDUS	MIDDLE	MINISTER		
II:	LITTLE				LONG					
III:	MILTON	MILTON	MONATIQUOT	MOUNT	MOUNTAIN	MUDDY	NEARY		NEPONSET	NEW

30)

I:	MINOR		MINOR			MINOR	MIRA	MOUND	MOUTH	MUZZLE	NAVEL
II:										LONG	LOVELL
III:	NEW	NORROWAY	NORROWAY	NOTCH	NORTH	NORTH	NORTH	NORTH			

31)

I:	NECK	NORTH	NORTHERN			NORTHERN	NOSE	NOSE	OFFICER	ONE
II:	LOWER	LOWER	MAFFIT	MARTIN				MARTINS		MATE
III:		NORTH	OAK		OLD	OLD	PAGE	PAROMET	PARK	PEARL	PEQUID

32)

I:		ONE	ONE	ONE	ONE	ONE	ONE		ONE	
II:			MIDDLE		MIDDLE	MOON	NANTASKET	NANTASKET		NARROWS
III:	PINE	PINE	PINE	PINE	PINNACLE	PLAIN	PLEASANT			

33)

I:	ONE		OPHIUCHUS	ORION	OSTRICHES	OUTSTRETCHED				
II:	NARROWS			NARROWS			NASH		NECK	NECK	NEPONSET	NIXES
III:	POND			POND			POND		POND		POND

34)

I:			PAN	PAN	PEACOCK	PEARLS	PEGASUS	PERSEUS		
II:	NORTHEAST	NUBBLE	NUT	OLD	ONE	OUTER	OUTER	PEDDOCKS	PHILIP	PIG
III:	POND	POND	POND	POND	POND	POND	POND	POND		POND

7

NAMES

								POINT		POLARIS
I	PERSEUS	PHOENIX						POINT		POLARIS
35) II	PINE			PLACE			PLEASURE	POINT		
III	POND	POND			PUDDIN	QUINCY	QUINCY		RADIO	RANDOLPH

I	POLLUX	PRINCE			PROUD	RAIN	RASTABAN	RAVEN	REAR	
36) II								POINT	POINT	POPE
III	RANDOLPH	RANDOLPH	RATTLESNAKE	REDWING	RIDGE	RIVER	RIVER	RIVER	RIVER	RIVER

I	REINHOLDER	RETURNING	RIDERS	RIDERS			RIGHT			RIGHT
37) II	PRESIDENT		PRINCE	QUARANTINE	QUARTER	QUARTER	QUINCY		RACCOON	RAGGED
III	RIVER	RIVER	RIVER	ROAD	ROAD	ROAD	-		ROCK	ROCK

I					RIVER	RIVER	ROARER			ROOT
38) II	RAINSFORD	RAM	RAM	REACH	REACH	RIVER	RIVER	RIVER	RIVER	RIVER	ROADS
III	RUN		RUN	SAINT	SAINT	SAINT	SAINT	SAINT		SAINT

I	ROTANEV		SABIK	SADDLE	SAGITTARIUS	SCALE	SCALE	SCREEN
39) II	ROADS	ROADS	ROARING	ROCK	ROCK	ROCK	ROCK	ROCK	ROCK
III	SAINT	SASSAMON	SCHOOL	SCHOOL	SCHOOL	SCHOOL	SCHOOL	SCHOOL	SCHOOL

I	SCORPIO	SEA	SECOND	SEGINUS	SEGINUS	SERPENT	SERPENT	SERPENTIS
40) II	ROCK	ROCK						
III	SCHOOL	SEMINARY			SEPULCHRE	SLIDE		SLIDE

8

NAMES

I	SERPENTIS		SHE	SHE	SHEPHERD	SHOULDER	SIDE	SIGN	SLAUGHTER	SNAKE
41) II									ROCK	ROCK
III	SKYLINE	SKYLINE	SOUTH		SOUTH	SOUTH		SOUTH	SOUTHEAST	SPRING

I			SNAKE			SNAKE		SNAKES	SOLITARY	SOUTH
42) II	ROCK			ROCK			ROCK		ROCK	ROCK
III		STOUGHTON		STREET	STREET	STREET	STREET	STREET	STREET

I		SOUTH	SOUTH	SOUTHERN	SOUTHERN	STAFF	STEWARD	STING	STING	SUALOCIN
43) II	ROCK		ROCK		ROCK	ROCK	ROCK	ROCK	ROCK	ROCK
III		STREET	STREET		STREET	STREET	STREET	STREET	STREET	STREET

I	SUHAIL		SWORD	TAIL	TAIL	TAIL	TAIL	TAIL	TAIL		TAIL
44) II	ROCKS	ROCKS	ROCKS	ROCKS	SACHEM	SAILOR	SCULPIN	SEA	SEAL	
III				STREET	STREET		STREET	STREET		STREET	STREET

I	TAIL			TARAZED	TAURUS	TAURUS	THE	THE	THE	THE	THIGH
45) II			SEAL		SEAL			SEAL	SHAG	SHEEP	SHOAL
III		SUNSET				SWAMP		SWAMP	SWAMP	THAYER

I		THRONE	TORTOISE	TOWER	TRAILING					TRIANGULUM	
46) II	SHOAL	SHOAL	SLATE	SOUND	SOUTH	SPECTACLE	SPIERS	SPIT	SPIT		SQUAW
III		THREE		TOWN	TOWER	TOWER	TOWER	TOWER	TOWER		TRAIL

9

NAMES

I		TRIANGULUM	TUCANAE	UPPER			URSA	URSA	VEGA	
47) II	STAND	STRAWBERRY	SUNKEN	TEWKSBURY	THIEVES			TUCKER	TUMBLING	
III	TRAIL	TRAIL		TRAIL	TREE		THIMBLE		THOMPSON	TURNPIKE

I		VENATICI	VIRGINS				VIRGINS		
48) II	THREE				TODDY			TOWN	
III	TURNPIKE	UNION			UNION	UNION	VALLEY	VERCHILD	WALE	WAMPATUCK

I		VIRGO	WAISTCLOTH				WEEPER	WEIGHT	WHALE	
49) II	TOWN			ULTONIA			UPPER	VEAZIE	WAY	
III	WAMPATUCK	WARD			WASHINGTON					WASHINGTON

I	WHEAT		WHIP					WING	WING		
50) II	WHIT	WELL	WEST	WEST		WESTERN	WEYMOUTH	WHITE		WORLDS	WRECK
III			WATER	WATER	WATER	WATER	WATER	WATER		WEST	WEST

70

NOTES ON THE PROPERTIES OF
WORDS

HOW SHALL WE DETERMINE THE METAPHORICAL OVERTONES OF NEIGHBORING WORDS? (THE CHINESE
WRITTEN CHARACTER AS A MEDIUM OF POETRY--FENOLLOSA/POUND)

INTERVAL--1.A- A SPACE OF TIME BETWEEN ANY TWO POINTS OR EVENTS ESPECIALLY BETWEEN
RECURRENT CONDITIONS OR STATES B- A PAUSE OR BREAK IN THE COURSE OF SOMETHING AS SESSIONS
C- A SPACE GAP OR DISTANCE BETWEEN OBJECTS STATES QUALITIES ETC 2.MUSIC- THE RELATION OF
TONES WITH REGARD TO PITCH (AN INTERVAL IS HARMONIC IF BETWEEN SIMULTANEOUS TONES
MELODIC IF BETWEEN SUCCESSIVE TONES)

INTERVALS BETWEEN WORDS IN A SERIES ARE COMPLEX RELATIONS OF SPELLING SOUND FORM MEANING
FUNCTION AND IDENTITY
RELATION OF WORDS WITH REGARD TO SPELLING: TO--TOO--TWO
RELATION OF WORDS WITH REGARD TO SOUND: THIN--THING--THINK
RELATION OF WORDS WITH REGARD TO FORM: GO--GOING--GONE
RELATION OF WORDS WITH REGARD TO MEANING: BLACK--GRAY--WHITE
RELATION OF WORDS WITH REGARD TO FUNCTION: I--READ--THIS
RELATION OF WORDS WITH REGARD TO IDENTITY:
SINGLE MEANING- YOU--YOU--YOU COMPLEX MEANING- SET--SET--SET

A SERIES OF WORDS CONTAINS AN ABSOLUTE STOCK OF DIFFERENT WORDS IF NO WORDS ARE REPEATED
THE ABSOLUTE STOCK CONTAINS THE SAME NUMBER OF ELEMENTS AS THE SERIES
THE INTERVALS BETWEEN WORDS ARE THE UNITS OF CHANGE FROM THE FIRST WORD TO THE LAST
IF WORDS ARE REPEATED THE SERIES CONTAINS MORE ELEMENTS THAN THE ABSOLUTE STOCK
UNITS OF CHANGE ARE REGULARLY DISTRIBUTED OVER THE ABSOLUTE STOCK IF WORDS ARE REPEATED
THE DISTRIBUTION OF THE UNITS OF CHANGE IS ALTERED BY THE DEGREE OF REPETITION
IF TWO OR MORE SERIES ARE READ SIMULTANEOUSLY INTERVALS ARE FORMED BETWEEN PARALLEL WORDS
SIMULTANEOUS READING OF TWO OR MORE SERIES FORMS GROUPS OF PARALLEL INTERVALS LET THESE
GROUPS OF PARALLEL INTERVALS BE CALLED INTERVALLIC SENTENCES
INTERVALS BETWEEN INTERVALLIC SENTENCES FORMED BY THE SIMULTANEOUS READING OF TWO OR MORE
SERIES OF WORDS ARE THE UNITS OF CHANGE BETWEEN THE FIRST AND THE LAST INTERVALLIC SENTENCES
PARALLEL SERIES OF WORDS CONTAIN AN ABSOLUTE STOCK OF DIFFERENT INTERVALLIC SENTENCES
UNITS OF CHANGE ARE REGULARLY DISTRIBUTED OVER THE ABSOLUTE STOCK OF INTERVALLIC SENTENCES
IF INTERVALLIC SENTENCES ARE REPEATED THE DISTRIBUTION OF UNITS OF CHANGE IS ALTERED BY THE
DEGREE OF REPETITION
SIMPLE REPETITIONS OF INTERVALLIC SENTENCES ARE FORMED BY THE PARALLEL REPETITION OF WORDS
IN THE SEVERAL VOICES
COMPLEX REPETITIONS OF INTERVALLIC SENTENCES ARE FORMED BY THE PARALLEL REPETITION OF WORDS
OCCURRING IN DIFFERENT VOICES AT DIFFERENT TIMES
SIMPLE REPETITIONS MUST BE CONSECUTIVE COMPLEX REPETITIONS MAY BE SEPARATED BY DISSIMILAR
INTERVALLIC SENTENCES COMPLEX REPETITIONS ARE PART OF THE ABSOLUTE STOCK OF INTERVALLIC
SENTENCES SIMPLE REPETITIONS CONSTITUTE ▮ THE DIFFERENCE BETWEEN THE WHOLE SERIES AND
THE ABSOLUTE STOCK OF INTERVALLIC SENTENCES.

ON THE SADNESS

The door is closed
We are going to die if the moon changes
The sky is blue then we are going to die if the grass is green
We are going to die then we are going to die if the sea is cold
The window is open
We are going to die if the sky is blue if men grow old
Night comes slowly
We are going to die then the sky is blue if the grass is green
The sky is blue if a girl sings
We are going to die if the sun is hot
Morning comes at five o'clock
We are going to die then we are going to die if the sky is blue
then we are going to die
The grass is green if men grow old
We are going to die if a boy runs
The sky is blue if the sea is cold
We are going to die then the grass is green
Fathers go to work
We are going to die if the sky is blue if the grass is green
Mothers mind their children
We are going to die then we are going to die if men grow old
The sky is blue then the sky is blue
We are going to die if a girl sings
The grass is green then we are going to die
We are going to die then the sky is blue if the sky is blue
The moon changes
We are going to die if the sea is cold
The sky is blue if men grow old
We are going to die then we are going to die if the grass is green
The sun is hot
We are going to die if the sky is blue then we are going to die
A boy runs
We are going to die then we are going to die then we are going
to die
The sky is blue if the grass is green
We are going to die if men grow old
A girl sings
We are going to die then we are going to die if the sky is blue
The sea is cold
We are going to die if the grass is green
The sky is blue then we are going to die
We are going to die then the sky is blue
Men grow old
We are going to die if the sky is blue
The grass is green
We are going to die then we are going to die
The sky is blue
We are going to die

1935	Born in Quincy, Massachusetts
1951-53	Studied with Patrick Morgan at Phillips Academy, Andover, Massachusetts Met Frank Stella, Hollis Frampton, and Michael Chapman
1954	Worked for Boston Gear Works Traveled to England and France
1955-56	Served in the United States Army as intelligence analyst
1957	Moved to New York
1958	Made first large wood sculpture
1960-64	Worked as railroad freight brakeman and conductor, Pennsylvania Railroad
1964	Work first exhibited, Yonkers, New York

CHECKLIST

Sculpture

1 Ladder # 1. 1958
Wood
68¾ x 8 x 8″
Hollis Frampton, New York

2 Plexiglas and Wood. 1958-59
Plexiglas and wood
12″ high; wood 2½″ wide, plexiglas 1½″ wide
Private Collection, New York

* 3 Wooden Piece. 1959
Wood
16 x 8½″
Barbara Rose, Madison, Connecticut

4 Pyramid. original 1959; reconstruction 1970
Wood
68⅞ x 31″
Courtesy George H. Andre, Orleans, Massachusetts

5 Cedar Piece. original 1959; reconstruction 1964
Wood
72 x 36¼ x 36¼″
Private Collection, New York

6 Untitled. 1960
Steel
9½ x 5″
Private Collection, New York

7 Untitled. 1961
Stainless steel, plate steel, and wood
24″ high
Lent anonymously

8 Steel Piece. Spring 1961
Steel
7 x 9½ x 2⅞″
Private Collection, New York

9 Hourglass. 1962
Wood
10 x 7″
Lee Lozano, New York

10 Cock. 1963
Wood
17 x 6 x 2⅛″
Lee Lozano, New York

* 11 Chain Sculpture. 1964
Wood and metal chain
42″ high; 23 units, each 3½ x 3½ x 18″
Collection The Aldrich Museum of Contemporary Art,
Ridgefield, Connecticut

12a Timber Piece. original 1964; reconstruction 1970
Wood
36 x 245 x 42″; 27 units, each 12 x 12 x 36″
Courtesy Dwan Gallery, New York

12b Timber Piece. original 1964; reconstruction 1970
Wood
84 x 48 x 48″; 28 units, each 12 x 12 x 36″
Courtesy Dwan Gallery, New York

13 Untitled. 1965
Cast cement
14 units, each 2¾ x 11 x 2¾″
Brandeis University Art Collection, anonymous gift

14 Equivalent. 1966
Sand lime bricks
5½ x 38⅝ x 48″; 120 units, each 2 x 6 x 10″
Mr. and Mrs. Manuel Greer, New York

15 Equivalent. original 1966; reconstruction 1969
Firebricks
5 x 108 x 22½″; 120 units
Lent by Dayton's Gallery 12, Minneapolis

16 Lever. original 1966; reconstruction 1969
Firebrick
4½ x 8⅞ x 348″; 137 units, each 4½ x 8⅞ x 2½″
Collection National Gallery of Canada, Ottawa

17 Reef. original 1966; reconstruction 1969, 1970
Styrofoam
25 units, each 20 x 108 x 10″
Heiner Friedrich, Cologne

* *Exhibited New York only*

† 18   Spill (Scatter Piece). 1966
Plastic and canvas bag
Dimensions indeterminant
Kimiko and John Powers, Aspen, Colorado

19   12 Pieces of Steel. 1967
Steel
180 x 20"; 12 units, each 20 x 15 x ⅜"
Mr. and Mrs. Robert A. Feldman, New York

20   Steel Piece. 1967
Steel
64 x 64 x ⅜"; 64 units, each 8 x 8 x ⅜"
Mr. and Mrs. Jan van der Marck, Chicago

* 21   144 Steel Plates. 1967
Steel
144 x 144 x ⅜"; 144 units, each 12 x 12 x ⅜"
Hessisches Landesmuseum en Darmstadt, Sammlung
Karl Ströher

22   144 Aluminium Plates. 1967
Aluminum
144 x 144 x ⅜"; 144 units, each 12 x 12 x ⅜"
Collection Pasadena Art Museum, California, anonymous gift

23   144 Zinc Plates. 1967
Zinc
144 x 144 x ⅜"; 144 units, each 12 x 12 x ⅜"
Milwaukee Art Center Collection, Wisconsin

* 24   Fall. 1968
Steel
72 x 540 x 72"; 21 units, each 72 x 28 x ½"
Courtesy Dwan Gallery, New York

25   144 Lead Plates. Spring 1969
Lead
144 x 144 x ⅜"; 144 units, each 12 x 12 x ⅜"
Collection The Museum of Modern Art, New York, Advisory
Committee Fund, 1969

26   144 Magnesium Plates. Spring 1969
Magnesium
144 x 144 x ⅜"; 144 units, each 12 x 12 x ⅜"
Mr. and Mrs. Thomas G. Terbell, Jr., Courtesy Pasadena
Art Museum

27   144 Copper Plates. Spring 1969
Copper
144 x 144 x ⅜"; 144 units, each 12 x 12 x ⅜"
Collection National Gallery of Canada, Ottawa

† Withdrawn from exhibition

28   64 Pieces of Copper. Spring 1969
Copper
64 x 64 x ⅜"; 64 units, each 8 x 8 x ⅜"
Private Collection, New York

29   Aluminum "Ribbon" Piece. Summer 1969
Aluminum
3¼ x 788¼ x ¹⁄₆₄"
Herman and Henriëtte van Eelen, Amsterdam

† 30   17 Steel Rod Run. Summer 1969
Steel reinforcing rods
¾ x 150¾"; 17 units, 7⅜, 10, 10, 11½, 10¼, 6¾, 6½, 8½,
10⅛, 7¼, 9, 11, 9¾, 10¾, 10½, 6⅜, 6¾"
Mr. and Mrs. Herbert Vogel, New York

31   Alloy Square. Fall 1969
Lead plates; aluminum plates
78¾ x 78¾"; 100 units
Konrad Fischer, Düsseldorf

32   37 Pieces of Work. Fall 1969
Aluminum, copper, steel, lead, magnesium, and zinc
432 x 432"; 1296 utis, 216 of each metal; each 12 x 12 x ⅜"
Courtesy Dwan Gallery, New York

Word Poems

33   Conquest Display. 1965
Collage
14 x 8½"
Mr. and Mrs. Ira Licht, New York

34   Touch Power. 1965
Collage
4⅛ x 8⅞"
Mr. and Mrs. Ira Licht, New York

35   Black Drown. 1965
Collage
22 x 19⅝"
Robert Hildt, New York

36   Structure White Consciousness. 1965
Collage
5¼ x 21⅞"
Mr. and Mrs. Michael Chapman, New York

37   Limbs. 1965
Collage
6½ x 7"
Mr. and Mrs. Herbert Vogel, New York

38 Bulk Cake. 1965
    Pencil on paper
    7¼ x 7″
    Mr. and Mrs. Robert A. Feldman, New York

39 Sum Toil. 1965
    Ink on paper
    3¼ x 5¼″
    Mr. and Mrs. Robert A. Feldman, New York

40 Turf Yard. 1965
    Ink on paper
    5 x 7¼″
    Mr. and Mrs. Robert A. Feldman, New York

41 Impulse Driver. 1965
    Collage
    5¼ x 7¾″
    Mr. and Mrs. Robert A. Feldman, New York

Operas

42 Flags. 1964
    Typed manuscript
    6 sheets, each 8½ x 11″
    Heiner Friedrich, Cologne

* 43 Names. 1964
    Typed manuscript
    9 sheets, each 8½ x 11″
    Courtesy Dwan Gallery, New York

* 44 Words (Preface). 1964
    Typed manuscript
    8½ x 11″
    Courtesy Dwan Gallery, New York

By The Artist

1 "Frank Stella", in *16 Americans*, The Museum of Modern Art, New York, 1959, p. 76.

2 *First Five Poems*, New York, 1961.

3 "Sensibility of the Sixties", *Art in America*, vol. 55, no. 1, January-February 1967, p. 49. Answer to a questionnaire by Barbara Rose and Irving Sandler.

4 "Novros", *57th Street Review*, April 1967.

5 "New in New York: Line Work", *Arts Magazine*, vol. 41, no. 7 May 1967, pp. 49-50. Statements by Brice Marden, Paul Mogensen and David Novros, compiled by Carl Andre.

6 "Letters", *Artforum*, vol. V, no. 10, Summer 1967, p. 4.

7 "Andre: Artist of Transportation", *The Aspen Times* (Colorado), July 18, 1968.
Interview by Dodie Gust (reprinted in bibl. 66).

8 "Artist Interviews Himself", in *Carl Andre*, Städtisches Museum, Mönchengladbach, Germany (see bibl. 63).

9 Untitled book, Seth Siegelaub/John W. Wendler, New York, 1968, n.p. Contributors: Carl Andre, Robert Barry, Douglas Heubler, Joseph Kosuth, Sol LeWitt, Robert Morris, Lawrence Weiner.

10 "Flags: An Opera for Three Voices", *Studio International*, vol. 177, no. 910, April 1969, p. 176.

11 "Time: A Panel Discussion", *Art International*, vol. XIII, no. 9, November 1969, pp. 20-23, 39. Transcript of a discussion held at the New York Shakespeare Theater, March 17, 1969; organized for the benefit of the Student Mobilization Committee to End the War in Vietnam; Seth Siegelaub, moderator; panelists included Carl Andre, Michael Cain, Douglas Heubler, Ian Wilson.

12 Seven books in a uniform manuscript edition of 36 signed and numbered sets, Dwan Gallery and Seth Siegelaub, New York, 1969. Includes *Passport*, 1960; *Shape and Structure*, 1960-1965; *A Theory of Poetry*, 1960-1965; *One Hundred Sonnets*, 1963; *America Drill*, 1963-1968; *Three Operas*, 1964; *Lyrics and Odes*, 1969.

13 "An Interview with Carl Andre", *Artforum*, vol. VIII, no. 10, June 1970, pp. 56-61. Interview by Phyllis Tuchman.

On The Artist

Books

14 Battcock, Gregory, ed., *Minimal Art: A Critical Anthology*, New York, 1968. Introduction by Gregory Battcock; essays by Michael Benedikt (reprinted from bibl. 74), Mel Bochner (reprinted from bibl. 30), David Bourdon (reprinted from bibl. 19), Michael Fried (reprinted from bibl. 27), E. C. Goosen (reprinted from bibl. 69), Clement Greenberg (reprinted from bibl. 79), John Perrault (reprinted from bibl. 24), Barbara Rose (reprinted from bibl. 16).

15 Celant, Germano, *Art Povera*, Milan, 1969.

Periodicals

16 Rose, Barbara, "ABC Art", *Art in America*, vol. 53, no. 5, October-November 1965, pp. 57-69 (reprinted in bibl. 14).

17 Richardson, John, "The Art Shops, The Cool School", *Sunday Times Magazine* (London), February 13, 1966, pp. 28-31.

18 Bourdon, David, "Our Period Style", *Art and Artists*, vol. 1, no. 3, June 1966, pp. 54-57.

19 Bourdon, David, "The Razed Sites of Carl Andre: A Sculptor Laid Low by the Brancusi Syndrome", *Artforum*, vol. V, no. 2, October 1966, pp. 14-17 (reprinted in bibl. 14).

20 Lippard, Lucy R., "Rejective Art", *Art International*, vol. 10, no. 8, October 1966, pp. 33-36.

21 Morris, Robert, "Notes on Sculpture, Part 2", *Artforum*, vol. V, no. 2, October 1966, pp. 20-23.

22 Bannard, Darby, "Present-Day Art and Ready-Made Styles", *Artforum*, vol. V, no. 4, December 1966, pp. 30-35.

23 Graham, Dan, "A Minimal Future? Models and Monuments: The Plague of Architecture", *Arts Magazine*, vol. 41, no. 5, March 1967, pp. 32-35.

24 Perrault, John, "A Minimal Future? Union Made: Report on a Phenomenon", *Arts Magazine*, vol. 41, no. 5, March 1967, pp. 26-31 (reprinted in bibl. 14).

25   Rose, Barbara, "Shall we Have a Renaissance?"
      Art in America, vol. 55, no. 2, March-April 1967, pp. 30-39.

26   Greenberg, Clement, "Recentness of Sculpture",
      Art International, vol. 11, no. 4, April 1967, pp. 19-21
      (reprinted from bibl. 79; reprinted in bibl. 14).

27   Fried, Michael, "Art and Objecthood", *Artforum*, vol. V, no. 10,
      June 1967, pp. 12-23 (reprinted in bibl. 14).

28   Morris, Robert, "Notes on Sculpture, Part 3", *Artforum*, vol. V,
      no. 10, June 1967, pp. 24-29.

29   Smithson, Robert, "Toward the Development of an Air
      Terminal Site", *Artforum*, vol. V, no. 10, June 1967, pp. 36-40.

30   Bochner, Mel, "Serial Art Systems: Solipsism", *Arts Magazine*,
      vol. 41, no. 8, Summer 1967, pp. 39-43 (reprinted in bibl. 14).

31   Davis, Douglas M., "The Dimensions of the Mini-Arts",
      Art in America, vol. 55, no. 6, November-December 1967,
      pp. 84-91.

32   Graham, Dan, "Carl Andre", *Arts Magazine*, vol. 42, no. 3,
      December 1967/January 1968, pp. 34-35.

33   Nylen, Leif, "Carl Andre", *Paletten*, no. 3, 1968, p. 28.

34   Van Schaardenburg, Lieneke, "Carl Andre: Ik Wil Uit De Tijd
      Zijn", *Vrij Nederland*, April 27, 1968, p. 12.

35   Burnham, Jack, "Systems Esthetics", *Artforum*, vol. VII, no. 1,
      September 1968, pp. 30-35.

36   Smithson, Robert, "A Sedimentation of the Mind:
      Earthprojects", *Artforum*, vol. VII, no. 1, September 1968,
      pp. 44-50.

37   Claura, Michel, "Andre", *Lettres Françaises*, no. 1251,
      October 1968, pp. 2-8.

38   Junker, Howard, "The New Sculpture: Getting Down to the
      Nitty Gritty", *The Saturday Evening Post*, vol. 241, no. 22,
      November 2, 1968, pp. 42-47.

39   Pleynet, Marcelin, "Peinture et Structuralisme", *Art
      International*, vol. 12, no. 9, November 1968, pp. 29-34.

40   Tillim, Sidney, "Earthworks and the New Picturesque",
      Artforum, vol. VII, no. 4, December 1968, pp. 42-45.

41   Muller, Gregoire, "In the Parisian Desert", *Arts Magazine*,
      vol. 43, no. 4, December 1968-January 1969, pp. 52-53.

42   Develing, Enno, "Kunst en Omgeving (Art and Environment)",
      Museumjournaal, vol. 14, no. 1, January 1969, pp. 2-9.

43   Rose, Barbara, "Problems of Criticism, V, Politics of Art,
      Part II", *Artforum*, vol. VII, no. 5, January 1969, pp. 44-49.

44   Kramer, Hilton, "The Emperor's New Bikini", *Art in America*,
      vol. 57, no. 1, January-February 1969, pp. 49-55.

45   Meadmore, Clement, "Thoughts on Earthworks, Random
      Distribution, Softness, Horizontality and Gravity",
      Arts Magazine, vol. 43, no. 4, February 1969, pp. 26-28.

46   Morris, Robert, "Notes on Sculpture, Part 4: Beyond Objects",
      Artforum, vol. VII, no. 8, April 1969, pp. 50-54.

47   Reise, Barbara, "Untitled 1969: A Footnote on Art and
      Minimal-stylehood", *Studio International*, vol. 177, no. 910,
      April 1969, pp. 166-172.

48   Pincus-Witten, Robert, "Slow Information: Richard Serra",
      Artforum, vol. VIII, no. 1, September 1969, pp. 34-39.

49   Novros, David, *Art Now: New York*, vol. 1, no. 8,
      October 1969, n.p.

50   Kosuth, Joseph, "Art After Philosophy Part II: 'Conceptual Art'
      and Recent Art", *Studio International*, vol. 178, no. 916,
      November 1969, pp. 160-161.

51   Battcock, Gregory, "The Politics of Space", *Arts Magazine*,
      vol. 44, no. 4, February 1970, pp. 40-43.

52   Burnham, Jack, "Alice's Head, Reflections on Conceptual Art",
      Artforum, vol. VIII, no. 6, February 1970, pp. 37-43.

53   Leider, Philip, "Literalism and Abstraction: Frank Stella's
      Retrospective at the Modern", *Artforum*, vol. VIII, no. 8,
      April 1970, pp. 44-51.

54   Nemser, Cindy, "An Interview with Eva Hesse", *Artforum*,
      vol. VIII, no. 9, May 1970, pp. 59-63.

One-Man Exhibitions and Reviews

55   Tibor de Nagy Gallery, New York, April 20-May 8, 1965.
      Announcement.
         T[ed] B[errigan], *Art News*, vol. 64, no. 4, Summer 1965,
         p. 21.
         Lucy R. Lippard, *Art International*, vol. 9, no. 6, September
         1965, p. 58.
         Jacob Grossberg, *Arts Magazine*, vol. 39, no. 10,
         September-October 1965, p. 72.

56   Tibor de Nagy Gallery, New York, March 29-April 16, 1966.
      Announcement.
         S[cott] B[urton], *Art News*. vol. 65, no. 3, May 1966, p. 14.

57   Dwan Gallery, Los Angeles, March 8-April 1, 1967.
      Announcement.
         William Wilson, *Los Angeles Times*, Part IV, March 24,
         1967, p. 2.
         Kurt von Meier, *Art International*, vol. II, no. 4, April 20,
         1967, p. 51.
         Jane Livingston, *Artforum*, vol. V, no. 9, May 1967, pp. 62-3.

58   Konrad Fischer Gallery, Düsseldorf, October 21-November 28,
      1967. Brochure.
         Hans Strelow, *Düsseldorfer Feuilleton*, no. 245, October 20,
         1967.
         Piero Gilardi, *Flash Art*, vol II, no. 6, January 15-February 15,
         1968, p. 2.
         John Anthony Thwaites, *Pictures on Exhibit*, vol. XXXI,
         no. 5, February 1968.

59   Dwan Gallery, New York, December 3, 1967-January 3, 1968.
      Announcement.
         John Perrault, *The Village Voice*, December 14, 1967, p. 19.
         Gordon Brown, *Arts Magazine*, vol. 42, no. 3, December
         1967-January 1968, p. 49.
         Al Brunelle, *Art News*, vol. 66, no. 9, January 1968, p. 11.
         F[elice] T. R[oss], *Pictures on Exhibit*, vol. XXXI, no. 4,
         January 1968, p. 18.
         Philip Leider, *Artforum*, vol. VI, no. 6, February 1968, p. 46.
         James R. Mellow, *Art International*, vol. XII, no. 2,
         February 1968, p. 73.

60 Galerie Heiner Friedrich, Munich, March 26-April 18, 1968. Announcement.

61 Wide White Space Gallery, Antwerp, May 4-25, 1968. Exhibition poster.

62 Munchener Gobelin-Manifaktur, Munich, September 20-October 16, 1968.

63 Städtisches Museum, Möchengladbach, Germany, October 18-December 15, 1968. Catalogue foreword by Johannes Cladders (on cloth); "Artist Interviews Himself", self-interview by Carl Andre (see bibl. 8), n.p.

64 Irving Blum Gallery, Los Angeles, December 3, 1968-January 3, 1969. Poster.
L[ois] D[ickert] Armstrong, *Art News*, vol. 67, no. 10, February 1969, p. 55.

65 Dwan Gallery, New York, April 26-May 21, 1969. Announcement.
John Gruen, *New York*, vol. 2, no. 2, May 19, 1969, p. 57.
Philip Leider, "To Introduce a New Kind of Truth", *The New York Times*, May 25, 1969.
John Perrault, *The Village Voice*, May 29, 1969, pp. 14-16.
Grace Glueck, *Art in America*, vol. 57, no. 3, May-June 1969, p. 118.
K[atherine] G. K[line], *Art News*, vol. 68, no. 4, Summer 1969, p. 12.
Peter Schjeldahl, *Art International*, vol. XIII, no. 7, September 1969, pp. 71-72.

66 Gemeentemuseum, The Hague, August 23-October 5, 1969. Catalogue essay by Enno Develing; poem preface by Carl Andre; letter to Enno Develing from Hollis Frampton; excerpts from "Andre: Artist of Transportation" (reprinted from bibl. 7); transcript of symposium at Windham College, Putney, Vermont, April 20, 1968.

67 Galleria Sperone, Turin, September 29-October 12, 1969. Announcement.

68 Ace Gallery, Los Angeles, February 7-28, 1970.
Peter Plagens, *Artforum*, vol. VIII, no. 9, May 1970, p. 83.

Group Exhibitions and Reviews

69 The Hudson River Museum, Yonkers, New York, *8 Young Artists*. October 11-25, 1964. Catalogue introduction by E. C. Goosen (see bibl. 14). Traveled to Bennington College Art Gallery, Bennington, Vermont.

70 Tibor de Nagy Gallery, New York, *Shape and Structure*. January 5-23, 1965. Announcement.
Vivien Reynor, *Arts Magazine*, vol. 39, no. 5, February 1965, pp. 53-54.
Barbara Rose, "Looking at American Sculpture", *Artforum*, vol. IV, no. 6, February 1965, pp. 29-36.

71 Westerly Gallery, New York, *The New Edge*. February 6-25, 1965. Brochure with biographies.

72 Institute of Contemporary Art, Boston, *Multiplicity*, April 16-June 5, 1966. Catalogue introduction by Molly Rannels.

73 The Jewish Museum, New York, *Primary Structures: Younger American and British Sculptors*, April 27-June 12, 1966. Catalogue intruduction by Kynaston McShine; bibliography by Katherine Kline.
Nan R. Piene, *Art in America*, vol. 54, no. 2, March-April 1966, p. 129.
Hilton Kramer, *The New York Times*, May 1, 1966, p. 23.
Max Kozloff, *The Nation*, June 6, 1966, pp. 693-694, vol. 202, no. 23.
Jay Jacobs, "Are They Trying to Tell Us Something?", *The Reporter Magazine*, vol. 34, no. 12, June 16, 1966, pp. 38-39.
Mel Bochner, "Primary Structures: Exhibition at the Jewish Museum", *Arts Magazine*, vol. 40, no. 8, June 1966, pp. 32-35.
Rolf-Gunter Dienst, "A Propos Primary Structures", *Arts Magazine*, vol. 40, no. 8, June 1966, p. 13.
Corinne Robins, "Object, Structure or Sculpture: Where are We?", *Arts Magazine*, vol. 40, no. 9, September-October 1966, pp. 33-37.

74 Dwan Gallery, New York, *10*, October 4-29, 1966. Illustrated catalogue.
Grace Glueck, *Art in America*, vol. 54, no. 5, September-October 1966, p. 105.
Peter Hutchinson, *Art and Artists*, vol. 1, no. 7, October 1966, p. 60.
Michael Benedikt, *Art International*, vol. X, no. 10, December 1966, p. 65 (see bibl. 14).
Annette Michaelson, "10 x 10: Concrete Reasonableness", *Artforum*, vol. V, no. 5, January 1967, pp. 30-31.
Traveled to Dwan Gallery, Los Angeles, May 1967.

75 Dwan Gallery, New York, *Scale Models and Drawings*, January 7-February 1, 1967. Poster.
P[atrica] S[tone], *Arts Magazine*, vol. 41, no. 4, February 1967, p. 57.
Dan Graham, "New York: of Monuments and Dreams", *Art and Artists*, vol. 1, no. 12, March 1967, pp. 62-63.
Robert Pincus-Witten, *Artforum*, vol. V, no. 7, March 1967, p. 52.

76 Ithaca College Museum of Art, New York, *Drawings 1967*, January 17-February 25, 1967. Catalogue introduction by Gretel Leed, Director; frontispiece by Daniel Gorski. Checklist, biographies.

77 Museum of Contemporary Crafts, New York, *Monuments, Tombstones, and Trophies*, March 17-May 14, 1967. No catalogue.
Ada Louise Huxtable, *The New York Times*, March 26, 1967, pp. 23-24.
J[eanne] S[iegel], *Arts Magazine*, vol. 41, no. 7, May 1967, pp. 54-55.

78 Park Place Gallery, New York, *David Novros*, April, 1967. Andre showed original version of REEF in back room. No announcement.

79 Los Angeles County Museum of Art, *American Sculpture of the Sixties*, April 28-June 25, 1967. Catalogue introduction by Maurice Tuchman, Curator of Modern Art; essays by Lawrence Alloway, Wayne V. Anderson, Dore Ashton, John Coplans, Clement Greenberg (see bibl. 14, 26), Max Kozloff, Lucy R. Lippard, James Monte, Barbara Rose, Irving Sandler.
Philip Leider, "American Sculpture at the Los Angeles County Museum", *Artforum*, vol. V, no. 10, Summer 1967, pp. 6-11.

Kurt von Meier, *Art International*, vol. XI, no. 6, Summer 1967, pp. 64-68.
Traveled to Philadelphia Museum of Art, September 15-October 29, 1967.

80 Bykert Gallery, New York, *Group*, May 16-June 17, 1967.
Lucy Lippard, "Rebelliously Romantic", *The New York Times*, June 4, 1967.
J[oseph] K[osuth], *Arts Magazine*, vol. 41, no. 8, Summer 1967, pp. 58-59.
H[arris] R[osenstein], *Art News*, vol. 66, no. 4, Summer 1967, p. 66.

81 Dwan Gallery, New York, *Language to be Looked At and/or Things to be Read*, June, 1967. Announcement.
Dennis Adrian, *Artforum*, vol. VI, no. 1, September 1967, p. 59.

82 Institute of Contemporary Art, Philadelphia, *A Romantic Minimalism*, September 13-October 11, 1967. Catalogue introduction by Stephen S. Prokopoff.

83 John Gibson Gallery, New York, *The Hanging Floating and Cantilevered Show*, November 11-December 31, 1967. Announcement.

84 Lannis Museum of Normal Art, New York, *Normal Art*, November 1967.

85 The Finch College Museum of Art, New York, *Art in Series*, November 22, 1967-January 7, 1968.
David Lee, *Art News*, vol. 66, no. 8, December 1967, pp. 42-45.
John Perrault, *The Village Voice*, December 14, 1967, p. 18.
Charlotte Willard, *The New York Post*, December 9, 1967, p. 12.

86 The Larry Aldrich Museum of Contemporary Art, Ridgefield, Connecticut, *Cool Art*, January 7-March 18, 1968. Catalogue introduction by Larry Aldrich.
J[ohn] S[amuels] M[argolies], *Arts Magazine*, vol. 42, no. 4, February 1968, p. 56.

87 Laura Knott Gallery, Bradford Junior College, Bradford, Massachusetts, *Carl Andre/Robert Barry/Lawrence Weiner*, February 4-March 2, 1968. Announcement with three unprinted pages for each artist. Symposium organized by Seth Siegelaub, February 8, 1968, including the three artists.

83 Gemeentemuseum, The Hague, *Minimal Art*, March 23-May 26, 1968. Catalogue introduction by Enno Develing; twenty paragraphs by Lucy Lippard; bibliography and biographies of each artist.
Enno Develing, *Museumjournaal*, vol. 13, no. 1, February 1968, pp. 2-12.
C. Blok, *Art International*, vol. XII, no. 5, May 1968, pp. 18-24.
A[nita] F[eldman], *Arts Magazine*, vol. 42, no. 8, June/Summer 1968, p. 57.
Traveled to Kunsthalle, Düsseldorf; Akademie der Kunst, Berlin.
Hanno Reuther, *Das Kunstwerk*, vol. XXII, no. 5-6, February-March 1969, pp. 74-75.

89 Stedelijk van Abbemuseum, Eindhoven, *3 Blind Mice/de Collecties: Vissers, Peeters, Becht*, April 6-May 19, 1968. Catalogue introduction by J. Leering and J. van de Walle.

90 Windham College, Putney, Vermont, *Exterior Situations*, May 1968. Symposium held on April 30, 1968, including Carl Andre, Robert Barry, Lawrence Weiner, and Douglas Heubler.

91 Fine Arts Galleries, University of Wisconsin, Milwaukee, *Art 1968: Hang Ups and Put Downs*, May 15-June 11, 1968. Illustrated checklist.

92 Dwan Gallery, New York, Language II, May 25-June 22, 1968. Announcement.
John Perrault, *The Village Voice*, June 13, 1968, p. 15.
John Chandler, "The Last Word in Graphic Art", *Art International*, vol XII, no. 9, November 1968, pp. 25-28.

93 Loeb Student Center, New York University, New York, *Art in Editions: New Approaches*, June 8-31, 1968. Catalogue essay by Louis Camnitzer.

94 Milwaukee Art Center, *Directions 1: Options*, June 22-August 18, 1968. Sponsored by the Joseph Schlitz Brewing Co. in conjunction with the Friends of Art for The Lakefront Festival of the Arts. Catalogue foreword by Tracy Atkinson; Introduction by Lawrence Alloway. Biographies. Statements by the artists.
Lawrence Alloway, "Interfaces and Options", *Arts Magazine*, vol. 43, no. 1, September-October 1968, pp. 25-29.

95 Galerie an der schönen Aussicht/Museum Fridericianum/Orangerie im Auepark, Kassel, *4. Documenta*, June 27-October 6, 1968. Catalogue foreword by Dr. Karl Branner. Essays by Arnold Bode, Max Imdahl, Jean Leering.
Jeanne Siegal, *Arts Magazine*, vol. 43, no. 1, September-October 1968, pp. 37-41.

96 Museum of Modern Art, New York, *The Art of the Real*, July 3-September 8, 1968. Catalogue introduction by E. C. Goosen. Bibliographies by Bernard Karpel.
Gregory Battock, "The Art of the Real: The Development of a Style: 1948-68", *Arts Magazine*, vol. 42, no. 8, Summer 1968, pp. 44-47.
Philip Leider, *Artforum*, vol. VII, no. 1, September 1968, p. 65.
Ralph Pomeroy, *Art and Artists*, vol. 3, no. 6, September 1968, pp. 54-56.
James R. Mellow, *Art International*, vol. XII, no. 8, October 1968, p. 60.
Traveled to Centre National d'Art Contemporain, Paris; Kunsthaus, Zurich, January 18-February 2, 1969.
Robert Kudielka, *Das Kunstwerk*, vol. XXII, nos. 7-8, April-May 1969.
Tate Gallery, London, April 24-June 1, 1969. Slight variation on New York catalogue; foreword by Gabriel White.

97 Kunsthalle, Düsseldorf, *Prospect 68*, September 20-29, 1968. Catalogue of gallery advertisements.
Rolf-Gunter Dienst, *Das Kunstwerk*, vol. XXII, nos. 1-2, October-November 1968, pp. 75-76.
Ed Sommer, *Art International*, vol. XIII, no. 2, February 20, 1969, pp. 32-35.

98 Dwan Gallery, New York, *Earthworks*, October 5-30, 1968. Announcement.
Grace Glueck, *Art in America*, vol. 56, no. 5, September-October 1968.

Peter Hutchinson, "Earth in Upheaval, Earth Works and Landscapes", *Arts Magazine*, vol. 43, no. 2, November 1968, pp. 19-21.
John Perrault, *The Village Voice*, October 17, 1968, p. 17.
Time, November 22, 1968, pp. 70-77.

99 Paula Cooper Gallery, New York, *The Artist for Peace*, October 1968. Organized by Lucy Lippard, Robert Huot, Ron Woland to benefit the Mobilization Against the War.
John Perrault, *The Village Voice*, October 5, 1968.

100 Neue Nationalgalerie/Munich. Neue Pinakothek, Berlin, *Sammlung 1968 Karl Ströher*, March 1-April 14, 1969. Catalogue essay by Hans Strelow.
Traveled to Kunstverein, Hamburg; Kunsthalle, Bern; Kunsthalle, Düsseldorf, April 25-June 17, 1969.
Klaus Honnef, *Das Kunstwerk*, vol. XXII, nos. 9-10, June-July 1969, pp. 61-62.

101 Stedelijk Museum, Amsterdam, *Op Losse Schroeven (Square Pegs in Round Holes)*, March 15-April 27, 1969. Catalogue introduction by E. E. de Wilde.
C. Blok, *Art International*, vol. XIII, no. 5, May 1969, pp. 51-53.
Klaus Honnef, *Das Kunstwerk*, vol. XXII, nos. 9-10, June-July 1969, pp. 62-63.
Tommaso Trini, "The Prodigal Maker's Trilogy", *Domus*, vol. 478, September 1969, pp. 45-46.

102 Kunsthalle, Bern, *When Attitude Becomes Form*, March 22-April 27, 1969. Catalogue foreword by John A. Murphy, President, Philip Morris Europe; exhibition sponsored by Philip Morris; Essays by Scott Burton, Gregoire Muller, Tommaso Trini. In collaboration with Institute of Contemporary Arts, London, September 28-October 27, 1969. Catalogue introduction by Harold Szeemann; revised catalogue essays by Charles Harrison, Scott Burton, Gregoire Muller, Tommaso Trini.
Jean-Christophe Ammann, "Schweizer Brief", *Art International*, vol. XIII, no. 5, May 1969, pp. 47-50.
Charles Harrison, "Against Precedents", *Studio International*, vol. 178, no. 914, September 1969, pp. 90-93 (reprinted from catalogue essay).
Bernard Denvir, *Art International*, vol. XIII, no. 8, October 1969, p. 72.

103 Hetzel Union Building Gallery, University Park, Pennsylvania, *Andre, Flavin, Judd, LeWitt and Morris*, April 6-May 20, 1969. Illustrated brochure.

104 John Gibson Gallery, New York, *Ecologic Art*, May 17-September 28, 1969. Announcement.
Lawrence Alloway, "The Expanding and Disappearing Work of Art", *Auction*, vol. III, no. 2, October 1969, pp. 34-39.

105 Paula Cooper Gallery, New York, *No. 7*, May-June 1969. Announcement. Organized by Lucy Lippard.

106 Whitney Museum of American Art, New York, *Anti-Illusion: Procedures/Materials*, May 19-July 6, 1969. Catalogue essays by James Monte and Marsha Tucker.
Peter Schjeldahl, *Art International*, vol. XIII, no. 7, September 1969, p. 70.
Emily Wasserman, *Artforum*, vol. VIII, no. 1, September 1969, pp. 57-58.

107 Gemeentemuseum, The Hague, *Carl Andre*, August 23-October 5, 1969. Andre's one-man show was his piece for group show organized by Seth Siegelaub, July-September, 1969. Exhibition catalogue with plans by each artist.

108 Seattle Art Museum, *557,087*, September 1969. Exhibition organized by Lucy Lippard; catalogue consists of notecards for each artist.
Traveled to Vancouver Art Gallery, January 3-February 18, 1970, *955,000*. Revised catalogue.
Peter Plagens, *Artforum*, vol. VIII, no. 3, November 1939, pp. 64-67.

109 Detroit Institute of Art, *Other Ideas*, September 10-October 19, 1969. Catalogue essay by Samuel Wagstaff.

110 Wide White Space Gallery, Antwerp, *Young American Artists*, September 20-October 19, 1969.

111 Kunsthalle, Cologne, *Kunstmarkt 1969*, October 14-November 9, 1969. Announcement.
R. G. Dienst, *Das Kunstwerk*, vol. XXIII, nos. 1-2, October-November 1969, p. 60.

112 Forth Worth Art Museum, *American Drawings*, October 28-December 9, 1969.

113 Ace Gallery, Vancouver, *Group*, November 1969.
Joan Lowndes, *Artscanada*, vol. XXVIII, no. 1, issue no. 140/141, February 1970, p. 47.

114 The Museum of Modern Art, New York, *Recent Acquisitions*, December 1, 1969-March 23, 1970. No checklist.

115 Paula Cooper Gallery, New York, *Drawings*, December 6, 1969-January 7, 1970. Announcement.

116 Art Gallery, University of California, Irvine, *Five Sculptors: Andre, Flavin, Judd, Morris, Serra*, December 9, 1969-January 18, 1970. Brochure.

117 Finch College Museum of Art, New York, *Art in Process IV*, December 11, 1969-January 26, 1970. Catalogue forward by Elayne H. Varian, statement by Carl Andre (reprinted from bibl. 7).
Philip Leider, *Artforum*, vol. 8, no. 6, February 1970, p. 70.

118 The Art Institute of Chicago, *69th American Exhibition*, January 17-February 22, 1970. Catalogue forward by Charles Cunningham; introduction by James A. Speyer.

119 Boston University of Fine and Applied Arts, Boston, *American Artists of the Nineteen Sixties*, February 6-March 14, 1970. Catalogue forward by Sidney Hurwitz; essay by H. Harvey Arnason.

120 The Art Museum, Princeton University, Princeton, New Jersey, *American Art in 1970*, May 5-27, 1970. Exhibition organized by Professor Sam Hunter's graduate students in American Art; no catalogue.

121 Dayton's Gallery 12, Minneapolis, *New Acquisitions*, May 6-June 6, 1970. Unnumbered catalogue.

122 Dwan Gallery, New York, *Language IV*, June 2-25, 1970. Announcement.

123 The Museum of Modern Art, New York, *Information*, July 2-September 20, 1970. Catalogue essay by Kinaston L. McShine.

PHOTOGRAPH CREDITS

Photographs of works in the exhibition:

R. Van Den Bempt (Courtesy Wide White Space Gallery): no. 29

Courtesy Dayton's Gallery 12: no. 15

Peter Dibke: no. 31

Courtesy Dwan Gallery: nos. 4, 11, 18, 19, 20, 42

Hollis Frampton: no. 7

Robert E. Mates and Paul Katz: nos. 1, 2, 3, 5, 6, 8, 9, 10, 12, 14, 17, 28, 30, 32, 33, 34, 35, 36, 37, 38, 39, 40, 41, 43, 44

Courtesy National Gallery of Canada, Ottawa: no. 16

Mike O'Neil: no. 13

Walter Russell (Courtesy Dwan Gallery): nos. 21, 22, 23, 24, 25, 26, 27

Photographs of works in the text:

Courtesy Dwan Gallery: pgs. 13, 14, 15, 16, 19

Courtesy Dwan Gallery and Seth Siegelaub: pg. 18

Foto Reproductie (Courtesy Haags Gemeente Museum): pg. 20

Hollis Frampton: pgs. 9, 10, 11, 12 right

Malcolm Lubliner Photography (Courtesy Ace Gallery): pg. 17

Robert E. Mates and Paul Katz: pgs. 12 left, 22

EXHIBITION 70/5

5,000 copies of this book designed by Malcolm Grear
have been printed by Joh. Enschedé en Zonen, Haarlem,
The Netherlands in September 1970 for the Trustees of
The Solomon R. Guggenheim Foundation on the occasion of
the exhibition
"Carl Andre"